D0076474

Facilitating Action Learning:
A Practitioner's Guide

Facilitating Action Learning:
A Practitioner's Guide

Mike Pedler and Christine Abbott

Open University Press

Open University Press
McGraw-Hill House
Shoppenhangers Road
Maidenhead
Berkshire
England
SL6 2QL

email: enquiries@openup.co.uk
world wide web: www.openup.co.uk

and Two Penn Plaza, New York, NY 10121–2289, USA

First published 2013

Copyright © Mike Pedler and Christine Abbott, 2013

A catalogue record of this book is available from the British Library

ISBN–13: 978–0–33–524597–0 (pb)
ISBN–10: 0–33–524597–8 (pb)
eISBN: 978–0–33–524598–7

Library of Congress Cataloging-in-Publication Data
CIP data applied for

Typesetting and e-book compilations by
RefineCatch Limited, Bungay, Suffolk
Printed and bound by CPI Group (UK) Ltd, Croydon, CR0 4YY

Fictitious names of companies, products, people, characters and/or data that may be used herein (in case studies or in examples) are not intended to represent any real individual, company, product or event.

The **McGraw·Hill** Companies

Contents

About the authors

Christine Abbott and Mike Pedler are partners in the Centre for Action Learning Facilitation (www.c-alf.org) which they founded in 2011. After many years of working with action learning as set advisers and as designers of programmes, they were sparked into this action by some powerful experiences in 2006/7 which raised the question: how can we know when we are 'doing it right'?

Mike Pedler is known for his work with action learning, the learning organization and leadership development. He is Emeritus Professor of Action Learning at Henley Business School at the University of Reading, Visiting Professor at Leeds Metropolitan and Sheffield Hallam Universities and Honorary Research Fellow at the University of Lancaster. He is Founding Editor of *Action Learning: Research & Practice* – the first international journal for action learning from Taylor & Francis/Routledge.

Christine Abbott is an action learning practitioner and academic. She is an associate of the Open University and Leeds Metropolitan University. Former Chairman, she is a Non Executive Board Member and Trustee of ILM. She co-wrote the qualifications for action learning that are on the OfQual framework. She has worked worldwide as an action learning practitioner and in the development of action learning set advisers.

Acknowledgements

We would like to acknowledge the many contributions to this work.

Chief amongst these are the people we have worked with as action learners, who have asked brilliant questions and written illuminative accounts of practice. Your enthusiasm and commitment have been central to making this book.

Thanks also to Kath and Roger for support and challenge in equal measure.

Introduction

We met in 1988 in an action learning set where Chris was a participant about to lose her job, and Mike was the facilitator. Twenty years later we worked together on a leadership programme where some action learning sets blamed their facilitators for not doing the job properly (Pedler and Abbott 2008a; 2008b). We were involved but also intrigued: as action learning advisers, how do we know when we are 'doing it right'?

This book arises from that question. After many years of working with action learning and mainly taking the set adviser role for granted despite Revans' warnings, we now felt differently. However popular the role now, it is not straightforward. Why is this? Let's start with Revans' lofty ambitions for action learning, as not just an approach to individual development but also a means of organizational and social renewal. The difficulties of this work are compounded when we find that Revans offers several definitions of what he takes to be the essence of action learning. This legacy leaves doubts which result in us asking ourselves questions about whether we are practising it appropriately. It seems that as action learning practitioners we must regularly be asking each other: 'am I doing it right?'

The growing demand for action learning in many different sectors around the world gives this question added importance. An 'action turn' is taking place in research in management and organizations which emphasizes the value of knowledge created in the context of action. Consequently, many, if not most, management, leadership and organization development programmes now incorporate some form of action learning.

And that word 'incorporate' brings more problems; the action learning philosophy of change and emancipation takes some fitting within the normal corporate frame. To take one example: if action learning is a prescribed methodology on these programmes, then in what sense are their participants 'volunteers'? The fifth of Revans' 'Characteristic assumptions of action learning' states that learning is voluntary (2011: 5). But have these participants been asked, invited or sent? The difficulties often start here. With true volunteers willing to give it a go, action learning is straightforward enough; but with pressed men or passive receivers the potential success of any endeavour must be in serious doubt. Thus the work of the action learning adviser begins well before any people have been invited or any set has been assembled.

Learning to do it right?

One consequence of action learning having no tight definition, is that there are many varieties in practice. This is not a simple methodology with fixed and universal procedures, but more an approach to learning and a working discipline based on some core values, which are applied differently by different practitioners. In many ways this is a good thing for it keeps action learning fresh and inventive, but there is a downside. Anyone can say they are doing 'action learning', and put this label on whatever they sell. We came across a recent example where someone had attended an 'action learning group' that consisted entirely of input from the manager, and in which the other participants had not had a chance to speak because 'there wasn't time'. In another instance, the participants brought their 'issues' or problems, but the facilitator did all the questioning, so as to 'model' this skill. Action learning sets may be almost compulsory on leadership development programmes these days, but are people really learning through taking action on 'intractable organizational problems'?

These uneasy feelings have been about for some time. Our particular concern is with the development of advisers or facilitators of action learning. The growth of action learning has sparked a demand for facilitators, and, in response to this demand, an outbreak of facilitator training courses. Whilst many such programmes help people with the skills of facilitation they tend to make the assumption that action learning is a form of small group work. We think that whilst action learning involves working in small groups or sets, it is far more than this. We also think that whilst there is no single right way to do action learning, and that, as David Casey put it, everyone has to 're-invent the wheel of their own practice', there are some right and wrong ways to go about it.

First, practising Revans' action learning needs a belief in the idea, and the understanding and ability to interpret it in local circumstances. In Revans' eyes, action learning is not a small group learning method but a means of organizational and social improvement. Whilst personal development is core to his vision, it is but one part of his theory of human action designed to bring about improvement of human systems, for the benefit of those who work in them, and are served by them. This means that as well as the skills of set advising, there are two other important sets of activities: the process of setting up and initiating action learning, and the sharing and spreading of learning in the wider organization or system.

To do this demanding work, the action learning practitioner needs their own means for continuing personal development. The habits of reflective practice and critical reflection are important both to keep ourselves honest and to produce quality work. But like any other action learner, an adviser will benefit greatly from peer support and supervision. The best source for this is the facilitators' or advisers' set which can provide a place where practitioners can ask each other 'Am I doing it right?'

Map of the book

The central idea in this book is that being an action learning adviser is not just about facilitating sets. In fact, our model (Figure I.1), suggests that this may be the most straightforward of three roles, and the one which is easiest to delegate to others. The book follows the sequence of this model, prefaced by an introduction to Revans' action learning and an overview of the three roles, and followed by chapters on critical action learning, on action learning as a more general way of working and on continuing practitioner development.

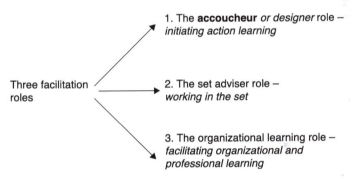

Figure I.1   Three roles of the action learning adviser

You are encouraged to use the book to answer your own questions as an active participant. Each chapter introduces ideas and concepts and offers opportunities to reflect critically on these in relation to your own practice. Reflecting on ideas and on your experiences and their implications for your practice can be enhanced through sharing with others. We suggest some ways of doing this in various chapters and we also have a website (*www.c-alf.org*) where you can also share your reflections and ideas.

The eight chapters are as follows:

1   *Action learning: its origins and principles* This introductory chapter tells the story of how the idea developed together with the core principles as proposed by Revans. Action learning is for tackling the 'wicked problems' of organizations and society as laid out in

the three systems of Alpha, Beta and Gamma – the decision or strategy system; the influencing or negotiation cycle and the learning process as experienced uniquely by each action learner.

As in all chapters, these ideas are illustrated with the help of case examples and activities that you can try for yourself. It closes with '*My practice notes*' – an invitation to reflect on the contents in relation to your own practice, which appear at the end of each chapter.

2   *Facilitating action learning – an overview* This chapter considers the facilitation challenge posed by Revans' radical ideas. The requirement for the set to be a peer learning community, and for members to be in charge of their own actions and learning, poses an intriguing challenge for any adviser. This chapter builds on the model introduced above (Figure I.1) and includes an overview of the three roles: the initiator or accoucheur, the set facilitator and the developer of wider organizational and professional learning, which are developed in the next three chapters. It also discusses the model of Self-Managed Action Learning and considers whether and how we can do without facilitators.

3   *The accoucheur: initiating action learning* The accoucheur role is the only aspect of the action learning adviser's job that receives Revans' explicit approval. Creating the right conditions is important in giving action learning a chance to work well; for example, agreeing the organizational challenges to be tackled, recruiting senior people to act as sponsors and clients and ensuring that set members are free to choose to join the sets. This initiation work is closely linked to the wider development in the system which is the third part of the adviser's role (Chapter 5). The accoucheur must design with organizational learning in mind, because this development depends heavily on the earlier work.

This chapter ends with the first part of Deller Business Services – an interactive case study in three parts – which appear successively in Chapters 3, 4 and 5. The Deller case depicts an action learning intervention in which you are invited to test your skills.

4   *The set adviser* The most familiar part of the adviser's role is working with the set to help it become a powerful and effective source of action, reflection and learning. This involves encouraging the development of key skills such as presenting issues, listening, questioning, reflecting and acting. This is mainly done through keeping the focus on the set and encouraging members to support and challenge each other. A key part of this aspect of the role is to progressively withdraw from the set as the members grow in confidence and begin to take on the facilitation functions

for themselves. This chapter also includes a section on Virtual Action Learning (VAL), which is an important new development in set advising. It concludes with the second part of Deller Business Services.

5   *The organization developer* This can be the most difficult aspect of the adviser's role, but it also carries the greatest potential for action learning. Revans' view of the organization was as a learning community where each member learned with and from the others. By acting between the set(s) and the sponsoring managers, the action learning facilitator can promote learning conversations which can lead to useful changes. This chapter contains cases, advice and activities for creating such 'middle-ground frameworks' and for promoting organizational and wider professional learning. The chapter also contains the last part of Deller Business Services, where you are invited to test your knowledge and skills in the action learning adviser's role.

6   *Becoming critical* Critical action learning (CAL) is an important development to help action learners stand outside their organizational and cultural surroundings to ask more fundamental questions. Because action learning is easily adapted to serve local agendas, in practice it often departs from Revans' foundational principles, and can end up maintaining the status quo rather than promoting learning and change. Critical action learning goes beyond 'ordinary criticality' to question existing practices, structures and power relations. It does this by distinguishing between effective practice, reflective practice and critically reflective practice. This chapter includes case illustrations and offers activities for practising CAL in sets, in order to help action learners become 'tempered radicals'.

7   *An action learning way of working* This chapter proposes action learning as a model for a wider way of collaborative organizing and working. Action learning sets encourage people to make connections across organizational and professional boundaries, and can make a contribution to 'social capital' in terms of the quality of relationships between people. Case studies and examples show how action learning can help in developing leadership, partnership working and networks. It is argued that the purpose, values and methods of action learning lend themselves to a vision for organizing where action learning is seen as a normal way of working. This is a long-term venture, but the ambitious action learning adviser is invited to see themselves as contributing to more effective organizing via the triple practices of facilitative leadership, network organizing and an action learning way of working.

8   *Developing your practice* The process of becoming an action learning adviser may include training or education but will always require a personal effort at self-development. By reflecting on their action and learning a person becomes able to describe their own practice, and to see how it can be improved. A model of *knowing, doing and being* is offered as a way of framing professional practice, and *the rhythm of professional development* – a cycle of experiencing, reflecting, reading and writing – is suggested as a means for continuing practice development. This last chapter also addresses the tasks of managing anxiety and power, with some ideas for reducing the former and a meditation on the latter. The chapter is illustrated with extracts from the accounts of practice of new action learning facilitators.

Key features of this book

- Action learning is presented, not as technique, but as a way of organizing and working together collaboratively.
- The adviser or facilitator role in action learning has three aspects: the accoucheur or initiator, the set adviser and the facilitator of organizational and social learning.
- There is an emphasis throughout on the idea of practice, with the reader encouraged to develop their own practice as a personal and professional accomplishment.
- Critical thinking and reflection are seen as vital in the development of practice in action learning.
- The style of the book aims both to be challenging and encouraging and to convey the spirit and philosophy of action learning.
- Each chapter combines ideas, models and activities for developing practice and suggestions for further resources and development.

1 Action learning: its origins and principles

Chapter overview

This chapter introduces the idea of action learning including the values and principles proposed by Revans. After discussing the origins of the idea in Revans' professional and personal life, his ambitions for action learning are laid out in the three systems of Alpha, Beta and Gamma: the decision or strategy system; the influencing or negotiation cycle and the learning process as experienced uniquely by each action learner. These three systems are illustrated with the help of a case example from a manufacturing company.

What is action learning for? *According to Revans, it is for tackling the 'wicked problems' of organizations and society rather than the puzzles which are the focus of much conventional education and training. And it cannot succeed in this purpose unless any such efforts are conducted in the light of certain critical values, which are discussed under the heading 'What is action learning really about?'*

The chapter closes by introducing 'My practice notes', which feature in every chapter. These are an invitation to reflect on what has been read by writing some notes on how this relates to your current practice.

This chapter contains:

- Introduction
- What is action learning?
- The origins of action learning
- The ambition of action learning
- What is action learning for?
- What action learning is NOT
- So, what is it really about?
- What has action learning become now?

- What does all this mean for the action learning adviser or facilitator?

- My practice notes 1

Introduction

Action learning originates with Reginald Revans (1907–2003) – Olympic athlete, nuclear physicist, educational reformer and professor of management (Figure 1.1).

Drawing on ancient sources of wisdom and more recent philosophers such as John Dewey, Revans sought the improvement of human systems by those who must live and work in them. Action learning suggests that we can address the most difficult challenges and problems through our own experiences and learning. Revans' idea is at one and the same time a pragmatic methodology for dealing with difficult challenges and a moral philosophy based on an optimistic view of human potential.

Figure 1.1 Professor R.W. Revans

What is action learning?

> 'There is no learning without action and no (sober and deliberate) action without learning'
>
> R.W. Revans 1907–2003

Revans never gave a single definition of action learning, and always maintained that there is no one form to what he described as ancient wisdom. The action learning *idea* is essentially simple, but its implementation and *realization* in the organizational and social world is anything but. Because it is concerned with achieving useful change and with the often profound learning that comes from being engaged in this process, it can never be communicated as a simple formula or technique.

However, many people are tempted to try to do just this. One of the main reasons for writing this book can be found in our amazement as what is currently described and sold as action learning. We are part of the movement to bring the action learning idea into practice in the world and our aspiration is to ensure that it is not sold short. Acknowledging that there is no one right or final way to describe action learning, here is our shot at describing action learning as it is currently applied in many settings today: 'Action learning is an approach to individual and organizational learning. Working in small groups known as "sets", people tackle important organizational or social challenges and learn from their attempts to improve things.'

This sounds straightforward enough, and it is: action learning brings people together to exchange, support and challenge each other in action and learning:

- First, each person joins and takes part *voluntarily*. (You can't be sent or send anyone else – although you might work at persuading and encouraging them.)
- Secondly, each person must own an organizational task, problem, challenge or opportunity on which they are committed to act.
- Thirdly, because we are very much more likely to succeed with the help of friends, action learning sets or small groups are formed to help each other think through the issues, create options and above all . . .
- Fourthly, take action and learn from the experience of taking that action.

These four elements are depicted in Figure 1.2.

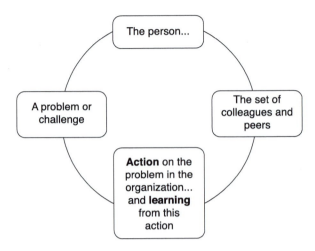

Figure 1.2 Four elements in action learning

The action learning set

The set is a very distinctive aspect of action learning. This small group meets regularly over time to help each other to act and to learn, and works on the basis of voluntary commitment, peer relationship and self-management. Revans described the set as: 'the cutting edge of every action learning programme' (2011: 10).

Figure 1.3 gives a depiction of a set at work. What do you see in the picture in Figure 1.3?

MANAGERS LIKE TO LEARN THROUGH EXPERIENCE

Figure 1.3 The action learning set

- These five people seem to be engaged in an experiment of some sort . . .
- It seems that they are trying to test some idea they have conceived but don't really know how to go about it . . .
- What is being attempted looks risky, there is the prospect of some danger, at least to the person tied to the top of the 'wheel' . . .
- Of the four people not at immediate risk, two seem to be pushing for the action, one seems to be in a restraining position, whilst the last seems to be observing and taking notes.

This is one picture of what an action learning set looks like in action. It helps its members to choose and tackle new challenges and to learn from the experiences arising from taking that action.

Revans trained as a physicist and brought the application of scientific method to the resolution of human problems. His crucial insight, which marks him off from most of his contemporaries and many thinkers today, is that the really difficult problems and challenges (those without right answers) are never resolved by experts (who deal in right answers) and can only be resolved by the people who actually have these problems and face these challenges. Resolving our own difficulties and improving our own systems is a difficult and daunting prospect and one we might often seek to avoid. But action learning suggests that with a little help from a few trusted friends, by working collaboratively we can begin work on inventing our own paths to the future.

The action learning set is to help each other to:

- make a voluntary commitment to work together on the 'intractable' problems or challenges of managing and organizing;
- choose problems or opportunities that personally engage the members of the set, so that they become those in which 'I am part of the problem and the problem is part of me';
- check individual perceptions of the problem, help to clarify them and render them more manageable, and also to create and explore options and alternatives for action;
- take action in the light of new insights gained from questioning and discussion in the set;
- support and challenge each other to act and learn effectively;
- reflect on and learn from the experiences of taking action by bringing back accounts of the action and its effects. Learning is first about the problem or opportunity being tackled; secondly it is about personal awareness – learning about oneself; and thirdly it is about the processes of learning itself or 'learning to learn'. (It

is the second and third of these types of learning that are essential for the transfer of learning to other situations.)

- acquire the skills of action and learning and become aware of group processes and what makes for effective teamwork.

That's about as much as you need to know about action learning in order to get on with it.

Revans was always very suspicious of people giving out too much theory or too many explanations; it was all so obvious to him – he wanted people to get on with it. Like eating ice cream or riding a bicycle, action learning has to be experienced. So, have a go and try it out, see how it works for you.

Finally, here's another definition of action learning from a doctor who was reflecting on her experience of working in a set (Box 1.1).

The origins of action learning

Action learning emerged as an important idea in the late 1960s. At this time and with the help of colleagues, Revans initiated two major projects: in a consortium of London hospitals (Wieland and Leigh 1971; Clark 1972; Wieland 1981); and in the UK's General Electric Company (Casey and Pearce 1977). Action learning was – and still is – an unusual innovation in organization development and management education because it is based on managers doing their own research and tackling their own problems. In championing the learners and doers it is opposed to expert consultancy and traditional business school practice.

In 1965, Revans resigned his professorship at the University of Manchester following his failure to influence negotiations over the new Business School, which he suggested should be based on action learning principles. Instead it was decided to build the Manchester Business School around the MBA, which was imported from the standard practice in US Business Schools. Revans left in protest at what he saw as the victory of the 'book' culture of the old University (Owens College) over the 'tool' culture of the College of Technology (later UMIST), which he saw as being closer to the needs of managers (1980: 197).

The action learning idea came to fruition over a long period of gestation and it was only in the 1970s, after leaving university life, that Revans first began using the term action learning. In a series of key books and papers beginning with *Developing Effective Managers* (1971), over the next ten years he laid out the theoretical and practical guidelines of what we now know as action learning. Revans' action learning is not just a new

Box 1.1 Recipe for successful action learning

Ingredients

- 6–8 people
- some tasks or problems
- commitment
- trust
- concern
- time
- experience
- support
- challenge
- risk
- facilitation
- humour

Method

Take a liberal slice of time, and mix thoroughly with the lifetime experience of several committed people. Sprinkle a generous helping of concern for others, and add enough trust to mould the mix until it jells firmly together. An added catalytic facilitator may help it to bind.

Season with a little risk. Add support and challenge whenever necessary. Leave to simmer indefinitely, stirring regularly as you feed in a variety of problems. An occasional dash of humour will prevent the mix from sticking.

Results

So what do you get? *Opportunities!*

- the opportunity to focus on particular areas of your professional life and to discuss at a level which, for a variety of reasons, you cannot do at work;
- the opportunity of new perspectives on such areas based upon the experience of others;
- the opportunity to develop and practise new skills in a relatively safe environment;
- the opportunity for reassurance that others have also 'been there before'.

. . . and friendship.

Source: Adapted from the original by Sheila Webb, Consultant in Public Health Medicine, Airedale

theory of management and organizational learning, but a philosophy for living and working based on strong ethical values. The importance of moral and ethical considerations is always apparent throughout Revans' writings, and his action learning is as much an ethos as it is a method.

Recent research (Boshyk et al. 2010; Boshyk 2011) suggests that Revans' early life experiences and personal development as a young man shaped the later development of his ideas in important ways. For example, there is an influence of Quaker values, perhaps from his family and certainly later from attendances at Quaker meetings in Cambridge in the 1930s when he was moving away from physics because of his doubts about being involved in research that could be used for aggressive purposes.

The similarities between Quaker belief and practices and action learning are quite striking. As Boshyk notes (2011: 89): 'Quakerism puts an emphasis on action or "practice", which takes precedence over belief, which "has meaning only in so far as it is enacted in practice".' Boshyk et al. (2010: 54–9) comment on the similarity between the workings of the traditional Quaker 'clearness committee' and the action learning set: any person seeking clearness on a deep personal problem or decision can call together five or six diverse but trusted people to help them find their inner voice. The clearness committee meets for about three hours, on one or more occasions, and starts with a 'centering silence'. Members do not speak to the focus person except to ask honest, caring questions to serve that person's need rather than their own curiosity. The clearness committee, dating back perhaps to the 1660s, was devised to draw upon communal wisdom to address the taxing problems of life, whilst acknowledging that these inevitably fall to individual responsibility and so must protect that person's integrity and essential self-direction from the risk of invasion by the judgements and beliefs of others.

Action learning, like the person calling clearness committee, starts in 'not knowing', or as Revans often said, unless we understand and acknowledge our own ignorance in the face of difficult problems, then we are not able to seek questions and learning. And there are other parallels between action learning and Quaker beliefs and practices: Quaker values include pacifism, equality, standing up to injustice and 'speaking truth to authority'; Quaker practice focuses on the importance of doubts and of the posing of questions and holds that quietness and reflection are essentials. Finally the strong belief in community resonates with Revans 'Comrades in adversity'.

The ambition of action learning

However, action learning was designed for an industrial society and for an age marked by the increasing predominance of large scale organizations. Behind the simple rules of action learning described in the first part of this chapter, Revans' thinking is based on what he called a 'praxeology' or 'general theory of human action' made up of three interacting systems: alpha, beta and gamma (Box 1.2).

Box 1.2 Revans' General Theory of Human Action – alpha, beta and gamma

alpha – *the strategy system* encompassing the external environment, the available internal resources and the managerial value system;

beta – *the decision system or negotiation cycle* required to implement the decision or strategy – of survey, trial, action, audit and consolidation;

gamma – *the learning process* as experienced uniquely by each action learner, involving self-questioning and awareness of self and others.

Source: Revans (1971: 33–67)

Alpha, beta and gamma are not easily separable in practice and are perhaps better seen as interacting parts of a whole. Taken together these three systems illustrate the scope and ambition of Revans' action learning:

- *System alpha is the source of the organizational problems to be tackled.* It sums up what Revans learned from his operational research phase in the 1940s and 1950s when he applied his scientific training to studies of mines, factories, schools and hospitals. The analysis of the external environment is necessary to reveal what opportunities and challenges may exist, whilst the inventory of internal resources is needed to see what may be deployed to exploit them.

   In adding the managerial value system to this orthodoxy of mainstream strategic thinking, Revans makes it clear that decisions are not just rational acts, but are contested and involve moral choices. System alpha is not just an intellectual analysis, but one which pays attention to history, cultures, power, politics and risk-taking in considering what different groups think ought to happen, and what they need to do about this.

- *System beta describes how the organizational problems should be tackled* via successive cycles of planning, action, reflection and learning. This, at the same time, is the cycle of scientific endeavour, the project cycle and also a 'cycle of institutional learning' (1971: 129). Addressing the problem involves an initial definition but also a negotiation of this meaning with important sponsors, clients, other actors and groups who are implicated or affected. The problem evolves as a result of learning from successive trials as options and opportunities for action emerge and effected.
- *System gamma is concerned with the personal learning of the individual* in their interactions with systems alpha and beta. All learning is voluntary, and how we learn from taking action on problems embraces both the person and the problem situation. It includes 'the effect of the change or action upon the manager, in one direction, and its complementary effect upon the situation, in the other' (1971: 54–5). System gamma recognizes that it is the individual who must make sense of the interaction of the three systems as the basis for their actions. Revans wrote of system gamma that it was: 'the essence . . . [it] represents in its own way the structure of all intelligent behaviour, and offers, in conjunction with systems alpha and beta, one starting point for a general theory of human action, for a science of praxeology' (1971: 58).

This general theory and its three systems set out the vision of action learning as a blend or admixture of individual action and learning, successive trials and cycles of experiment and wider systems change. Revans' thinking prefigures the interest in the learning organization and organizational learning which emerged some 20 years later.

This brief sketch of Revans' ambitions for action learning also serves to frame the challenge for the action learning adviser or facilitator: to achieve these aims calls for far more than the facilitation of small groups. Facilitating sets is but a small part of the picture, as the example from John Tann Security shows (Box 1.3).

Box 1.3 John Tann Security

Colin, John, Les and Pete were senior line managers at John Tann Security Ltd., a heavy fabrication company making safes, vaults and security equipment. They formed themselves into a management action group with the help of an external adviser.

The company was faced with a number of problems including small batches, high product variety and changing fashions in the market for security equipment. The directors wanted to increase output and efficiency and also develop the management potential of their key people. Unusually perhaps, they also felt that 'often good ideas in a company do not originate at Board level'. They wanted to establish an environment in which 'ideas would flow upwards through the company structure'.

The four managers met weekly with the external adviser over six months and worked well as a team. At the last meeting they reviewed their success together with their sponsoring director. Unusually however, they did a second review four years later (all of them were still working in the company) and evaluated the benefits under four headings:

1 *Productivity* – over the four years productivity improvement was +11%, +19%, +17% and +13% (the original target = 15%). Whilst not stemming entirely from the action learning, this was seen as the major factor.

2 *Individual management development* – the four managers believe that the action learning experience 'was the most significant factor' in establishing better decision making, more delegation, less defensive attitudes and improved ability to take criticism, improved self-confidence and leadership, proper application of disciplinary procedures and the ability to confide in their director in the belief that 'he wanted them to manage and would allow them to do so'.

3 *Team building* – they now operate as a much more effective team.

4 *Continuing use of action learning* – the four formed a set for their deputies and shared the role of adviser in order to pass on what they had learned. This set was not so successful; it met for several meetings but then petered out. The four managers put this down to the presence of one of themselves as part of the company hierarchy and the absence of an external adviser.

Source: Adapted from Brown (1991)

What is action learning for?

The John Tann example illustrates several of the purposes of action learning. Action learning is for tackling the really difficult challenges and problems facing us as managers and citizens, but it is also a profound source of personal development. The 'principle of insufficient mandate' holds that unless we can change ourselves we cannot change anything that goes on around us (Revans 2011: 75–6), or to put it another way round, when we set out to change things in the world and we do this from a starting position of openness to learning then we also find ourselves changed in the process. The four John Tann managers are developing themselves as persons as well as managerially by tackling the productivity and other challenges of their organization.

Colin, John, Les and Pete set up their group because they sensed that they needed to learn in order to resolve the problems facing the company. Revans' change equation holds that:

$$L \geq C$$

which means that people, organizations or societies only flourish when their learning (L) is at least equal to, or better still, greater than, the rate of environmental change (C). He further suggests that adults learn by combining what we already know with fresh questions about what we do not know. His learning equation holds that:

$$L = P + Q$$

so that learning is a combination of P (*programmed knowledge*), or what we already know; and Q (*questioning insight*), which is inspired by fresh questions about the challenges where we do not know and do not have solutions. The element of Q is the key to the distinction Revans makes between:

PUZZLES and PROBLEMS

Puzzles have 'best' solutions and can be solved by applying P with the help of experts. Revans uses the word 'problems' to describe situations where there are no right answers and which are best approached through questioning which provokes new lines of thinking, action and learning. Action learning is not designed for puzzles, which are 'difficulties from which escapes are thought to be known', but for situations where 'no single course of action is to be justified . . . so that different managers, all reasonable, experienced and sober, might set out by treating them in markedly different ways' (Revans 2011: 6).

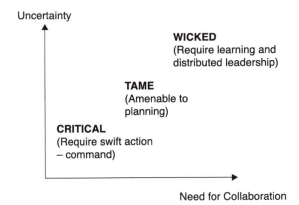

Figure 1.4   Three types of problem

Source: Grint (2008)

Another name for this sort of challenge is 'wicked'. Grint's (2008: 11–18) leadership model (Figure 1.4) has three sorts of problems and the progression from 'critical' to 'tame' to 'wicked' shows up in increases in uncertainty about solutions and the much greater need for collaboration. *Critical* problems such as heart attacks, train crashes or natural disasters demand swift action, leaving little time for procedure or uncertainty. Although *tame* problems such as planning heart surgery or building a new hospital can be very complicated, they are 'tame' because they are amenable to the tools of rational planning. Wicked problems defy rational analysis and require *leadership and learning*. Wicked issues are messy, circular and aggressive. Eliminating drug abuse, homelessness or crime in a neighbourhood; motivating people; developing entrepreneurship or working across boundaries in organizations are all tricky in this way. Simple strategies and straightforward actions often lead to unintended consequences due to the complex interdependencies of issues and stakeholders on site.

Action learning is the process intended for such wicked issues: proceeding by questions, by not rushing to solutions, by learning from making deliberate experiments and deliberated risks.

What action learning is NOT

Revans is famous for saying what action learning is not (2011: 62–74) rather than what it is. It is NOT 'Project Work, Case Studies, Business Games and other Simulations. Group Dynamics and other Task-free

Exercises, Business consultancy and other Expert Missions, Operational Research, Industrial Engineering, Work Study and Related Subjects' nor even 'Simple Commonsense'. Revans concludes his review of what action learning is not, by saying that:

> action learning is less structured than these other approaches . . . It makes little use of teachers, specialist and other professional sclerotics, and tries to encourage the managers themselves, those who have to take the decisions about their own tasks, to discover how best to help each other.
>
> (2011: 74)

On the other hand, it also follows from his account that there may be many efforts at organizational improvement that can achieve action learning. Call them 'quality circles', 'productivity improvement teams', 'action inquiry groups' or whatever you wish. It matters little what a group is called (the naming should fit the circumstances); the acid test is whether the people concerned are helping each other to take action on their problems and challenges, and whether they are learning from this work.

Indeed, one of the strengths of action learning is that, being never defined once and for all, it must be re-interpreted or re-invented to fit the present conditions. This means it is never in danger, as fixed techniques often are, of being popular today and forgotten tomorrow. The basic ideas are simple, but we always need to craft the practice and fashion our own ways of applying them. This inventing element is what maintains the life and vitality of action learning.

So, what is it really about?

Tackling difficult challenges and wicked problems is perhaps demanding enough, and yet there is more. Revans was passionate in encouraging people to help themselves, and also urged us to help those who cannot help themselves (1982: 467–92). Action learning is founded on an uncompromising moral philosophy about how to be and how to act. Whilst the action learning 'rules of engagement' are easily understood, they have to be enacted via these moral values:

- *starting from ignorance* – from acknowledging inadequacy and not knowing;
- *honesty about self* – 'What is an honest man, and what do I need to do to become one?' (Belgian manager quoted in Revans 1971: 132);

- *commitment to action, and not just not thought* – 'be ye doers of the word, and not only hearers of it' (St. James quoted in Revans 2011: 6);
- *in a spirit of friendship* – 'All meaningful knowledge is for the sake of action, and all meaningful action for the sake of friendship' (John Macmurray quoted in Revans 2011: 6);
- *for the purpose of doing good in the world* – 'To do a little good is better than to write difficult books' (The Bhudda quoted in Revans 2011: 6).

In action learning, and in contrast to other learning theories, spirit, heart and courage are as important as intelligence and insight. In challenging situations, the warmth and support of friends and colleagues are as vital as their knowledge and critique. We return to the importance of these values in Chapter 7.

Box 1.4 Nine ways to kill action learning!

Action learning is a powerful approach and discipline for personal and business development. However, success is not guaranteed. Here are a few of the ways in which you can stop action learning working:

- Come along when you don't really want to
- Come without a real issue to work on
- Bring something along that you already know how to do
- Keep quiet about your real issues – don't give anything away
- Turn up infrequently to meetings
- Don't take any action between set meetings
- Talk about other members and their issues outside the set
- Give everyone the benefit of your advice at every opportunity
- Use the set meetings to score points and show how clever you are

Do any or all of these and you are sure to have a deadly impact!

What has action learning become now?

Since its appearance in the 1960s and 1970s, action learning has been controversial in promoting learning over teaching, and championing practitioner knowledge over that of experts. There has been a substantial growth of action learning activity since the 1980s and it is perhaps closer now to the 'mainstream' than at any other time in its history. There are two main reasons for the growth of activity:

- *The use of action-based approaches in corporate programmes* Leadership development programmes in large organizations are reported as increasingly using approaches such as coaching, work-based learning, problem-based learning and action learning.
- *Interest from academics and universities* This partly reflects the increased corporate usage which creates opportunities for research and practice-oriented postgraduate programmes. Academic interest comes both from organizational researchers interested in 'actionable knowledge' (Coghlan 2011), and from those looking for a more critical business and management education (Trehan 2011).

Alongside this growth of use and interest, action learning itself is changing. This is evident in both how it is practised, and in how it is perceived:

- *As a family of approaches* Action learning has spread as an idea rather than as a specific method, and whilst there is agreement on the key features of the idea, there are wide variations in its practice (Pedler et al. 2005: 64–5). These variations can be seen either as departures from 'Revans Classical Principles' or as developments of them. For example, much current practice focuses on 'own job' projects and personal development, rather than on organizational problems, and can therefore lose what is vital in Revans' vision. However, there are also new practice developments which he could not have envisaged, such as virtual action learning (VAL). Because different practice communities have developed their own versions of action learning this means that it is sensible to think of it not as a unitary practice but as a family of approaches.
- *As a member of the family of action-based approaches to research and learning* More broadly, action learning is also part of a wider growth of action approaches to management and organizational research, which aim to produce 'actionable knowledge'. These include action research, action science and participative action inquiry amongst others with similar perspectives.

What does all this mean for the action learning adviser or facilitator?

There is a lot to take in here and at least as many ways of playing the facilitator role as there are of interpreting action learning. As we shall see in the next chapter, Revans did not pay a great deal of attention to the role of facilitator and rather distrusted people who assumed this status. This causes a number of problems for people who take on this role, especially as there is not one single definition of what action learning may be, so there is no one right way to facilitate. This means that every facilitator of action learning is condemned to be continually asking the question: am I doing it right?! (Pedler and Abbott 2008).

You make like to record your reflections so far in *My practice notes*.

My practice notes 1

My practice of action learning

Write yourself some notes on action learning as it relates to your current practice. Record your thoughts on these questions:

1   What do I make of action learning as an idea?

2   Does it fit with my current skills set?

3   What do I value most about action learning? Is it something that fits with my personal values?

4   Which aspects of action learning practice to I want to develop next?

Reflection on *My practice notes* 2:
Reading through what I have just written, what does it say about me and my practice?

2   Facilitating action learning: an overview

Chapter overview

This chapter considers the facilitation challenge posed by Revans' radical ideas. For situations in which there are no right answers, action learners are encouraged to avoid the advice of experts and to seek advice first from their peers and fellow set members. The requirement for the set to be a peer learning community, and for set members to be in charge of their own actions and learning, poses an intriguing challenge for any facilitator. The trick for the facilitator is to be helpful without succumbing to an expert role thus taking the power and focus away from the set members.

Preceding and following on from the questions of set facilitation are two other groups of challenges concerning: first, the initiation of action learning and the creation of the right organizational conditions for success; and secondly, the harvesting and dissemination of organizational and professional learning.

This chapter provides an overview of these three main aspects of the action learning adviser's role: the initiator or accoucheur, the set facilitator and the developer of wider organizational and professional learning. It also considers the model of self-managed action learning which Revans often seemed to prefer – and discusses the development of the action learning adviser.

This chapter contains:

- Introduction
- Revans on facilitation
- The three roles of the action learning adviser:
  - the accoucheur
  - the set adviser or facilitator
  - the developer of organizational and professional learning
- Self-managed action learning
- The irresistible rise of the facilitator

- Learning to become an action learning adviser
- My practice notes 2

Introduction

Definitions of action learning don't usually mention the adviser or facilitator role – it is the set, the set members, the challenges being tackled and the learning from this action that are important.

Although the role of the facilitator is now considered to be important, it had no place in Revans' early descriptions of action learning. The set adviser or facilitator role dates from the mid-1970s, when Revans was working alongside others including David Casey, David Pearce, Jean Lawrence and Bob Garratt on the pioneering programmes established in the UK's General Electric Company (Casey and Pearce 1977).

Since this time, and despite Revans' misgivings and frequent warnings, the role has usually been seen as a critical component of action learning. The popularity of the set advising role can be ascribed to a number of possible reasons including the commonly accepted view that such specialists can add value to the workings of a set, especially in the early stages, to the more cynical perspective that action learning provides attractive career development for erstwhile teachers and trainers. Revans did accept the role somewhat reluctantly as detailed below, but he always preferred the term 'adviser' to emphasize its advisory and non-executive status. By contrast he made frequent injunctions against the language of facilitation – which can be read literally as making things easy – which no experienced adviser would ever promise. He even lampooned the term facilitator, once dubbing it 'fer-silly-taters'.[1]

One by-product of the widespread usage of the facilitator in action learning programmes has been the frequent appearance of accounts of this role, its skills and practices. Many authors have assumed it to be a specialized form of small group facilitation; although from this starting point, interpretations can proceed in quite different directions. McGill and Beaty (2001) and McGill and Brockbank (2004) for example emphasize the value of interpersonal and reflective skills in the facilitator and especially the understanding of group dynamics in the set. Marquardt (2004; 2009) on the other hand makes his facilitator an activist 'coach' who takes a strong lead in questioning and guiding members in their learning.

1 For any non-Northerners, 'taters' = potatoes.

In our view the set facilitator or set adviser role is but one part of a much wider action learning adviser role. We also think that it has been over-emphasized at the expense of other, more important and more challenging aspects. Our position is based on Revans' ambition for action learning, involving as it does, action and learning on the intractable problems facing communities, organizations and societies – a task that requires much more than the facilitation of small groups. To realize his vision a different perspective is needed on the role of the adviser in action learning.

In this book we use both the terms 'adviser' and 'facilitator'. Whilst 'facilitation' and 'facilitator' are by far the much better known terms, they are also mainly used in the context of meetings and projects where the intentions and dynamics are different to those of action learning. In line with this common usage, we use the terms facilitator, facilitation and facilitating especially in relation to working with the action learning set.

Revans on facilitation

Revans' ideas about the education of managers represent a radical challenge to traditional business school practice. When, in 1965, the London and Manchester Business Schools were being established, their offer to managers was based (as now) on the MBA model. Revans was strongly opposed to this import from the USA because of its unquestioning reliance upon received wisdom and expert knowledge. Instead, he said, the focus should be on helping managers themselves *to learn how to solve problems* (1966: 5; 1980: 197).

Revans saw an important role for the adviser in introducing action learning to organizations and in helping the sets to get started. However, he had doubts fearing that the role of facilitator would become an expert role in itself. He foresaw that management teachers might soon begin to call themselves facilitators, and whilst this was to be welcomed if it was a genuine conversion, he feared that they would not change their spots and would continue, under a new guise, to deploy their expert roles. Because of this, he was at pains to stress that action learning set members, individually and collectively, should control their own affairs, so as to avoid *'yet another round of dependence upon ambiguous facilitators'* (2011: 9, original emphasis).

The three roles of the action learning adviser

However, a further analysis of Revans' thoughts on the role of the action learning adviser reveals three important aspects or parts of this role (Figure 2.1).

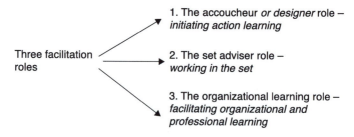

Three facilitation roles

1. The accoucheur *or designer* role – *initiating action learning*

2. The set adviser role – *working in the set*

3. The organizational learning role – *facilitating organizational and professional learning*

Figure 2.1   The three roles of the action learning adviser

The accoucheur

Revans recognized the importance of someone to introduce action learning to any organization or system. To help with the introduction and induction processes he used the term 'accoucheur': 'No organisation is likely to embrace action learning unless there is some person within it ready to fight on its behalf. . . . This useful intermediary we may call the accoucheur – the managerial midwife who sees that their organisation gives birth to a new idea' (2011: 98–9).

However, Revans envisaged this role as being carried out by a sympathetic manager. He thought that this task of introducing action learning was one best suited to a senior person in any given system or organization, and not as work for outside professionals.

The set adviser or facilitator

Whilst giving most legitimacy to the accoucheur role, Revans noted that when it comes to the point of the sets beginning to meet: 'there may be a need when it [the set] is first formed for some supernumerary . . . brought into speed the integration of the set'. But, so concerned is he about the dangers of opening the door to such expert professionals that he quickly attaches the rider: 'Such a combiner . . . must contrive that it [the set] achieves independence of them at the earliest possible moment' (2011: 9) and goes on to suggest that the job is probably best done by another manager with some personal experience of action learning rather than any outside professional:

> . . . [F]or a newly assembled set any need for an integrating agent, to encourage among its mutually unacquainted members as quickly as possible the ease and familiarity essential to self-disclosure, can be met, not by engaging some professional 'facilitator' but by inviting an active manager, who has himself

been through an exercise in action learning already, to work with the new group for long enough to get them going. It is possible he might want to join them as a substantive member . . .

(1982: 769)

Revans perhaps hopes here, that the manager, being unpaid and likely to have other work to do, will not be inclined to hang around unnecessarily and, as soon as possible, will either leave the set to get on with the work themselves, or that they will join the set as an ordinary member.

Many action learning advisers try to observe Revans' guidance in this respect, especially those who propose the self-managed action learning approach (SMAL – see below). The SMAL approach is close to Revans' own vision for the set; that, with a little help, encouragement and instruction, the members will soon acquire the skills and confidence sets to facilitate themselves.

To sum up his views as best we can, Revans saw an important role for the set adviser in introducing action learning to organizations and in helping the sets to get started. His problems with the set facilitation aspects of the adviser's role were twofold:

- The presence of such an authority figure conflicts with the notion of an autonomous set and can prevent it becoming a peer learning community. Revans was critical of an educational culture that he saw as dominated by authority and dependency, and thought that managers were most likely to learn 'with and from each other' (1982: 767–8).
- Whatever their good intentions in helping the set become independent of them, facilitators will be seduced by the power of the role, and retain their expert status in the set.

His position on the facilitation role in sets can be summed up in three injunctions:

- Peers are the best consultants. We need to talk to each other – as equals – about our issues and questions.
- Facilitation can be useful in helping people to get started on action learning, but . . .
- Beware of all 'experts' – especially including expert facilitators!

The developer of organizational and professional learning

Once action learning is established, with sets up and running and with members engaged in action and learning on their chosen issues, the question arises of how does any host organization or wider system benefit from these efforts?

In addition to any substantive gains from problem solving and project work, Revans describes 'the multiplier effect' as action learners address their issues and share their findings in a wider 'learning community' (2011: 70–3). How is this to be brought about?

In his reflections on working with managers in Belgian companies he discusses the difficulties of communication and the problems of access to authority which are essential to bring about systemic change. To deal with these difficulties he proposes the formation of 'key groups' of the people outside the sets, who are most likely to be affected by any proposed actions and without whom local action is likely to fail (1971: 80–94). Later he calls this a structure of welcome, which is to be built within a system, via the development of sponsors, clients, client groups and 'supporting assemblies' (2011: 21–39). These welcoming structures serve not only to support the action learning process, but also to facilitate organizational learning.

Revans obviously understood that, without this support from leadership, the weight of expectations on individual set members to make an organizational impact would be too great. Yet, it is not clear who he expected to do this work of forming key groups and facilitating supporting assemblies. In some projects he did this work himself, or relied upon resident management developers who may have invited him in in the first place. His basic position is that all managers should take on this responsibility for bringing about the learning community, starting at the top. Thus, in his blueprint for an organization which is able to learn, his first prescription is: 'That its chief executive places high among their own responsibilities that of developing the enterprise as a learning system' (2011: 117).

It is sometimes argued that Revans' ambition for organizational change and learning puts too much pressure on participants, or that it is simply too difficult and time consuming. Additionally, 'organizational change' is not the largely rational process that Revans sometimes appeared to imagine, and the issue of organizational learning turns out to be a complex and contested matter. Subsequently, given that there is already so much change and turmoil, some action learning practitioners have suggested what we really need is not more initiative taking but more reflective space for sense making and critical appraisal (Rigg 2008). The important development of *critical action learning* discussed in Chapter 6 is part of this shift in focus.

Where the emphasis is on the facilitation of action learning sets, and concerned with the development of members via 'own job' problems, attention is likely to be focused on the face-to-face processes of facilitation in the set and less on organizational action and learning. A different sort of facilitation is required to bring about a dialogue between action learners and those responsible for the overall direction and leadership in a system.

This suggests three tasks for the action learning adviser: advising the set, engaging the leadership and facilitating the conversation between the first two. Working within the set is the most familiar of these tasks but possibly the least demanding (see Figure 2.2).

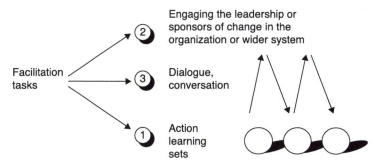

Figure 2.2 Facilitating organizational learning

Professional learning

The third aspect of the adviser's role encompasses organizational learning as in Figure 2.2, but can also be extended to the development of wider professional learning. Whilst organizational development in some circumstances and conditions may be felt by some to be too demanding or beyond their remit, the responsibility for wider professional learning should arguably not be beyond any practitioner's remit.

Those people engaged in action learning tend to be skilled or professional workers with numerous links and allegiances to professional bodies, forums, networks and communities of practice. 'Knowledge workers' and other professionals are inclined to replenish and update their knowledge in networks, communities of practice and forums of peers. Informal professional gatherings and networks play a significant part in disseminating and sharing learning. Here people can not only agree on best practices but also share those tacit understandings and insights which cannot be codified in procedure. Additionally many trades and vocations have a tradition of concern with ethical practice and professional development, which is enshrined in associations and institutions which carry and safeguard these concerns. These bodies may themselves be important providers and sources of learning, and are not infrequently the organizers of the more informal forums and networks.

These formal and informal gatherings create an opportunity for wider professional learning. Taking insights from action learning processes into these wider circles of influence is an important task for both action learning set members and advisers. It may well prove to be an easier and more natural route for the dissemination of new intelligence than attempts to exchange learning with senior managers who may be resistant to new knowledge which conflicts with their current understandings. However, this should complement rather than replace the effort at organization development. As Revans noted in his most succinct summary of the learning organization, senior managers become wiser by information reaching them from below: 'Doubt ascending speeds wisdom from above.'

The development of organizational and professional learning poses a timely challenge for the action learning adviser. Today, in much current practice action learning has become a method for personal development, analogous to coaching or mentoring, its only distinction being that it is done in 'sets'. This is a pale shadow of what Revans envisaged, and is, on its own, unlikely to result in the systemic improvements in organizations and societies that he sought. As Donnenberg argues, this individualizing of action learning can work against wider learning: 'Individualistic learning is detrimental to connectivity ... Within the fragmented organization of a hospital with its many subcultures there is a great need for integrating the many efforts to the advantage of the patients' (2011: 301). Whilst achieving this connectivity and integration is an intimidating challenge for any adviser, what remains of the action learning vision without it? We return to this important topic in Chapter 5.

Self-managed action learning

Can we do without facilitators?

Revans' warnings about the set facilitator role prompt an obvious question: can we do without facilitators?

Because of Revans' concession that sets need external facilitation at the start, many advisers and facilitators have taken the view that a key part of the task is to enable the set to become self-facilitating. Once this has been achieved, the adviser should then leave the set. But, whilst espousing this theory, many practitioners have ended up staying with their sets, and have shown a marked reluctance to make themselves redundant. Nancy Dixon describes eloquently how this may happen:

> Ideally, a facilitator models the skills . . . for a period of time and then works himself out of a job as soon as possible as members of the group take over the facilitation role themselves. However, the reality is that both the facilitator and group members tend to hang on to the status quo. For the facilitator it is very difficult to relinquish such an attractive role as the 'wise and insightful'. Especially when others come up to you afterwards and say 'I'm really glad you said that in the group'. Or 'I don't know how you see those things that just go over the heads of the rest of us'. Who wouldn't want to hang on to such a valued role?
>
> (in Bourner 2011: 114)

The case for SMAL has been argued by Tom Bourner and his colleagues, who have demonstrated its effectiveness in a number of large scale programmes involving hundreds of managers (Bourner 2011). The practice of SMAL is arguably truest to Revans' vision of the peer learning process. Its distinctive features are:

- After some preparatory workshops, the action learning sets are self managing and self-facilitating.
- 'Self-management' is the preferred overall term because it encourages set members to use their existing managerial skills, thereby building confidence in their own abilities; and also because it demystifies the facilitation process.
- SMAL emphasizes membership skills – presenting issues, questioning, summarizing, reflecting, coaching one another, and . . .
- de-emphasizes facilitation by an external, specially-skilled person.

Being an effective set member

The focus on self-management and the set members' skills leads to a clear script for the conduct of action learning sessions (see Box 2.1).

Box 2.1 SMAL: being an effective set member

Taking your turn and presenting issues:

- Prepare for the meeting by thinking about what you want to achieve from your time. What do you need from the set today?
- Think about how much you need to say to explain how things are going.
- Explain this as clearly as you can. (Sometimes you may want to ask the set to help you think through something you feel confused about.)
- Try to stay within your time limit.
- Point out to the set what is not helpful to you.
- Develop action points . . .
- Work on them before the next meeting and . . .
- Reflect on your learning and share it with others.

When listening, questioning and supporting others:

- Keep the focus on the person who is presenting and on their learning.
- Listen actively.
- Stick to the ground rules and challenge others if they do not.
- Be supportive – show interest and empathy.
- Learn not to interrupt.
- Ask helpful questions.
- Ask for clarification.
- Be honest, open and specific in your feedback while being sensitive.
- Treat diversity and equality issues seriously.
- Provide information if requested.
- Offer insights and ideas tentatively and at the right time.
- Take responsibility for your own learning.
- Collaborate with others in their learning.
- Speak for yourself.
- Avoid sweeping generalizations.
- Accept that someone else's solution may be different from your own.

And attend all the meetings and stay from beginning to end.

Source: Adapted by K. Aspinwall from Beaty et al. (1993)

SMAL is a very useful contribution to action learning methodology because it can be employed in any set to build up the skills of members in order to help them become autonomous and free-standing. It can also be utilized by advisers and facilitators to free up their time for the wider organizational tasks. Thirdly, the emphasis on membership skills promotes action learning as a general way of meeting and working beyond the boundaries of the set and in the wider system. Many action learning set advisers may see their work exclusively in terms of facilitating the set but there is plenty of other, perhaps more important, work to do. In the SMAL programmes described by Bourner and his colleagues, the action learning advisers are busy on a number of tasks linked to the 'accoucheur' role described earlier; setting up the programmes, creating 'supportive assemblies', running preparatory workshops, holding conferences to bring sets and sponsors together, evaluating outcomes, acting as consultants to sets and occasionally facilitating a set meeting.

The irresistible rise of the facilitator

Despite the contribution and example of SMAL, most action learning sets continue to have facilitators, and most accounts of action learning assume the presence of this role (O'Hara et al. 2004; Pedler et al. 2005). Possible explanations for this include Revans' own predictions that, as action learning grew in popularity, it would attract professional teachers and trainers seeking to reinvent themselves as facilitators. Whilst he was sceptical about this move, fearing that such people would merely assume their expert roles in new guise, there are reasons to be more optimistic. First, many educators and trainers come to action learning looking for alternative and better ways of working. Both they and their clients have come to see the limitations of traditional teaching and training approaches, and seek to make use of approaches that put the learner and learning at the centre of their practice.

A second reason for the ubiquity of the facilitator is the paradox that, whilst action learning is a simple enough idea, it is not always so simple to put into practice. Revans makes action learning sound straightforward – get half a dozen managers together to help each other to act on, and learn from, tackling organizational problems. But, for example:

- How do people come together in sets within organizations, or between organizations? Are they volunteers? Are they free to say no?

- Where do the organizational problems come from? Who says they are problems? What sort of agreement or contract exists between the action learners and their clients and sponsors on the definition of these problems?
- And what does it mean to act on an organizational problem? How likely are the set members to risk themselves in this way? What counts as action? And how is the 'risk imperative' – the existence of a significant risk of penalty for failure (Revans 2011: 6) – realized in practice?

These are just some of the challenges to be dealt with to bring out the full potential of action learning. Seen in this light, the action learning adviser's role is a very much more demanding one than that of the facilitator of managerial meetings, where an external person is called in to help a group or team with their tasks. As the name implies, the role of the facilitator here is to *make easier and help* (the team) *move forward* with their tasks.

The facilitators of management gatherings and project teams may think their jobs hard enough, but their remit normally ends with the meeting or series of meetings. For effective action learning, as we have seen, the adviser should not only help the set members learn with and from each other whilst tackling difficult organizing tasks, but also, in line with Revans' injunction *Outwards from Set to Learning Community* (2011: 70–3), help them with the wider responsibility to influence people outside the set and promote learning in the organization and in wider professional forums.

Learning to become an action learning adviser

The starting point for this book is the question of how someone might best learn to become an action learning adviser. Skills with small groups are arguably useful but scarcely adequate to the task. The 'skilled facilitator' might cause you, like the small boy with the hammer, to hit everything you come across with the same tools. In action learning there is always this injunction to start by asking fresh questions, from a position of not knowing how to proceed.

The 'My practice notes' found in each of these chapters are invitations to develop the good learning habits which will help with any practice. Reflection and writing down are one important way of developing this practice of the action learning adviser. Yet there is no substitute for doing the task and learning from that experience.

Revans' word 'praxeology', from the Greek *praxis*, means the study of practice, including the interaction of thinking and doing. Revans' motivation was to help managers 'learn how to solve problems' (1966: 5), and so the notion of practice is central to action learning. Practice implies doing and learning, and doing these at the same time:

> A man *may well learn to talk about taking action simply by talking about taking action* (as in classes at a business school) but to learn *to take action* (as something distinct from learning to talk about taking action) then he needs *to take action* (rather than to talk about taking action) and to see the effect, not of talking about taking action (at which he may appear competent) but *of taking the action itself* (at which he may fall somewhat short of competent).
>
> (Revans 1971: 54–5, original emphasis)

This is very different in tone to the training language of 'skills' and 'competencies'. For example, what Revans is saying is that whilst skills imply ability, they do not necessarily lead to action; competencies refer to past learning, but they do not speak of the need for the new.

Our practice is what we deploy in the face of difficult situations; at the same time it is the foundation and the focus for new learning. In one version of his three systems, alpha, beta and gamma, Revans (1982: 724) reprises them as changes in three sets of relationships, with:

- the external world,
- other practitioners, and . . .
- with oneself.

Alpha, beta and gamma thus stand for three levels of practice that connect the person with a wider community, and with wider challenges in the world:

- MY practice: my personal way of working
- OUR practice: the professional community of practice
- THE practice: a recognised service for particular human purposes.

  (Pedler et al. 2010: 10)

We come back to this important theme in Chapter 8. You might like to make some notes for yourself on these three roles of the action learning adviser as they apply to your practice.

My practice notes 2

The three roles of the action learning adviser

Write yourself some notes on these three roles as they relate to your current practice. For example, you might want to record your thoughts on such questions as:

- *Is this a part of what I do now? Should it be?*

- *Which of these three do I find more difficult or intimidating?*

- *Which appeals to me most?*

- *Which of these is a priority for me at the moment?*

- *Which one would I most like to develop?*

1   *The accoucheur*
2   *The set facilitator*
3   *The organizational learning adviser*

Reflection on *My practice notes 2*:
Reading through what I have just written on these three roles, what does it say about me and my practice?

3 The accoucheur: initiating action learning

Chapter overview

The accoucheur role may be neglected for the more immediate returns of set advising. Yet the success of any action learning initiative depends upon this work – the only one of the three roles to receive explicit approval from Revans.

To give action learning a chance to work well, it is useful to first test the climate of welcome in any organization or system. If the system is able to host action learning, then the best chance of success lies in preparing the right conditions, including the engaging of top leadership support and the recruitment of some senior people to act as sponsors and clients. This is the accoucheur's job, along with agreeing on how the organizational challenges are to be chosen and making sure that people are free to choose to join as set members, rather than being drafted in.

This initiation work is closely linked to any subsequent organizational development in the system, and which makes up the third part of the action learning adviser's role (Chapter 5). The accoucheur anticipates the prospects for organizational development in laying the groundwork for any wider learning. And, although the accoucheur and the organization developer roles are split in this book by the second role of the set adviser (Chapter 4), this only makes sense chronologically, because these first and third aspects of the action learning adviser's role are a joint endeavour. The accoucheur must design with organizational learning in mind, and the achievement of any wider development beyond the sets depends heavily on this work.

This chapter considers the reconnaissance, contracting and design aspects of the accoucheur role, offers advice on recruitment of members, choice of problems and some initial thoughts on evaluation and gives case examples of action learning programmes in large and small organizations.

It also contains the first part of Deller Business Services – a case study in three parts – which appear successively at the end of Chapters 3, 4 and 5. The Deller case depicts an action learning intervention in a large enterprise, and you are invited to test your knowledge and skills in the action learning adviser's role as the case develops.

This chapter contains:

- Introduction
- Organizational readiness
- Is there support and commitment from the top?
- Designing action learning
- Who should be the set members?
- How should be challenges and problems be selected?
- An action learning programme
- Evaluating action learning
- My practice notes 3
- Case study: Deller business services – Part 1

Introduction

As we saw in the previous chapter, Revans' doubt about facilitators stemmed from his concern that people taking on this role would also take on the mantle of knowers of how to do action learning, and would therefore become experts in their own right, defeating the principle of peer advice.

The dilemma is that there is an obvious need for someone to introduce action learning to any new group or organization. In the early days Revans did this himself, but as the idea spread, how were these action learning introduction and induction processes to be achieved? He used the term 'accoucheur' – literally (male) midwife – to emphasize that this role was needed before and at the birth, but not after the healthy child was born. However, as we said in the previous chapter, he thought that this work might be best done by an enlightened manager in the organization concerned, rather than any professional facilitator.

The accoucheur is the first of three roles of the action learning adviser (see Chapter 2, Figure 2.1) and it has close links with the third – the facilitator of organizational learning. The success of that last, and in many ways, most important role, depends on the groundwork done by the accoucheur, who must design with organizational learning in mind, and this possibility depends heavily on the good work which is done from the very beginning of the process.

It is the initiator who will first plant the seeds of the action learning idea; who will set the tone, define the concept and set out its ambitions.

It will be in this pioneering work that relationships are made with senior managers and leaders, clients, sponsors and other stakeholders. Together with any other 'key groups' and 'supporting assemblies', it is from these people that the 'Structure d'Acceuill' or structure of welcome for action learning in that organization or system, is built (Revans 1971: 80–94; 2011: 21–39).

It is obvious that the spade work done with these people and groups is core to success of the action learning effort including any organizational learning that is accomplished. It is the influence upon, and he activities of, all these people *outside the set* which make up what Revans described as the 'multiplier effect' as learning is shared in a wider 'learning community' (2011: 70–3).

The accoucheur role includes an important design element. In all probability, it is to this person that client organizations will turn to propose the design for any action learning venture. This design role can be easily underestimated as it requires no less than the translation of the apparently simple principles of action learning into complex contexts: how will people be invited and find their way into sets? Who will be chosen and invited? How will the challenges and problems be chosen? How will progress be evaluated? and how will learning be shared? In all these questions the devil is likely to be in the details. It is at this point that the radical intent and values of action learning come up against the existing culture and values of the host organization.

Creating the right conditions for action learning is the key task of the set adviser as accoucheur and initiator. This includes asking such questions as:

- How will this organization or system welcome action learning activities?
- Will it be supported by top management?
- How will people be made aware, invited and recruited?
- How will problems or challenges be chosen?
- Will participants have clients, sponsors or mentors?
- Will there be any supporting activities to run alongside the action learning sets, such as visits, meetings or seminars with external people?
- Is there any plan to follow up and take advantage of any momentum created by the action learning sets?
- How will any learning be shared in the wider organization or system?

These questions attest to the amount of foundational work that may be involved with establishing a successful action learning initiative. All this comes before any set advising work can happen. If this is done well then the set adviser's or facilitator's task is made much easier. If the preparation is not done well, then action learning may not work as wished or promised.

This chapter reviews these questions, offers a strategic overview of the initiation process and points to further resources and activities for more detailed design work.

Organizational readiness

The idea of organizational readiness can be simply expressed in the following questions:

- Do you really want to do it?
- Is this organization ready for action learning?

An ideal state of organizational readiness is the situation where there is enough openness and support to give action learning the space and permission to thrive whilst offering sufficient challenge to the existing order to provoke change and learning.

Action learning is not for everyone, nor for all organizations, at all times. If you have a lot going on in your life, now may not be a sensible time. Companies that do lots of training do not necessarily welcome action learning. Action learning needs the chance to work on significant organizational problems and opportunities, together with people who are willing to have a go. Have you got enough of this? If the climate or culture of an organization or system is hostile to action learning, or cannot host it well enough to give it a good chance of working, then it might be better to seek options outside that system.

There are conditions, especially in young pioneering projects, where action and learning are so uninhibited, so natural a part of the way things are done, that action learning happens as a matter of course. People point out problems as they see them and offer help readily to others without embarrassment. It is delightful and exciting to be in such situations, where everyone puts their shoulder to the wheel as necessary, and where everybody shares in the learning and the progress. However, such ideal states often do not last. As organizations get older, bigger and more managed, they tend to lose the natural ability for action and learning. They become more formal; people have to ask for permission for innovations, and may be punished for making mistakes, and as a consequence everyone becomes more risk averse. If things have not gone too far, and there is still the opportunity of open-mindedness at senior levels, then action learning can help to loosen things and encourage people to innovate and experiment with new ways of working.

In deciding whether action learning will work in this or that situation, consider the following:

- Does the idea fit with the stage of development of the organization?
- Are people ready to take more initiative, have more of a say, be entrepreneurial, take risks, run their jobs as if they were their own small businesses?

The Organisational Readiness for Action learning Questionnaire (see Figure 3.1) will help you assess your situation. You can use it by yourself, as an aid to thinking, or with colleagues to pilot the idea and check collective judgement on whether it 'has legs' in this situation, or you can use it as a survey instrument to assess the potential for action learning in any team, project, department or community.

The Organisational Readiness for Action Learning Questionnaire will help you assess the chances of success for action learning in your situation.

For each statement score the organisation from 1 (not much like us) to 5 (very like us):

IN THIS ORGANISATION . . .

. . . people are rewarded for asking good questions

1 2 3 4 5

. . . people often come up with new idea

1 2 3 4 5

. . . there is fairly free flow of communications

1 2 3 4 5

. . . conflict is surfaced and dealt with rather than suppressed

1 2 3 4 5

. . . we are encouraged to learn new skills

1 2 3 4 5

. . . we take time out to reflect on experiences

1 2 3 4 5

. . . there are plenty of books, films, packages and other resources for learning

1 2 3 4 5

. . . people help, encourage and constructively criticise each other

1 2 3 4 5

... we are flexible in our working patterns and used to working on several jobs at once

1 2 3 4 5

... senior people never pull rank and always encourage others to speak their minds

1 2 3 4 5

NOW TOTAL UP YOUR SCORE, IF YOU SCORED . . .

... between 10 and 20	Action learning probably won't work very well until things open up a bit more.
... between 21 and 40	Yes – action learning should work well to help you achieve your purpose.
... over 40	You don't seem to need action learning! ... or perhaps action learning would help develop your critical and questioning faculties?

Figure 3.1   The Organisational Readiness for Action Learning questionnaire

Source: Reprinted with permission from Pedler (2008)

Is there support and commitment from the top?

Action learning is likely to have the biggest impact on people and on their organizations if it has support from powerful people. *The Organisational Readiness for Action Learning Questionnaire* will help in estimating the climate or mood of any group that is sampled, but some other questions are indicated when considering the extent of interest, support and commitment from the top managers:

How can action learning

- support their visions and aims?
- offer ways forward on some of their organizational problems and issues?

Selling action learning to senior people often involves making a business case for the commitment of resources and energies which addresses these issues. A third question may have to be estimated rather than directly answered:

- To what extent, will they sponsor change, experiments and the questioning of current practices?

Getting support and commitment from senior people in the system is more or less essential for the prospects for organizational learning. Action learning can happen in organizations without this support, but the benefits tend to be limited to the sets, and to the individuals in them. In some cases action learning even happens without the knowledge of the top managers, as in the 'shadow side' case in Box 3.1. In this case, the action learning effort is hidden from the view of those at the top and might even be seen as subversive of their purposes. And yet, even in the shadow side of the organization, action learning could still find a place to work and be of value at least to individuals. Also, despite the leadership being kept in the dark, at least two arguments can be made for the value to the organization of this 'subversive' activity: first, and directly, through helping the company to retain its new graduates; and secondly, but more indirectly, because all organizations

---

Box 3.1 Case example: Action learning on the 'shadow side'

The management development manager of a large international but family-owned firm, was concerned about the recent graduate intake. As the company had grown, it had not changed its management style and was privately described as 'feudal' at times.

Several of the recent graduates taken on just a few months previously had come to the management development manager with their concerns about their jobs, their bosses and how they were being treated. He decided to respond by organizing – without the knowledge of his superiors – an action learning set for seven of the most fed-up trainees. At the first meeting, after discussions about ground rules and confidentiality, all those present said that they wanted to leave the company and asked the set and the management development manager for practical help to this end.

After eight fortnightly meetings, two of the new graduates had indeed left the company, but others had found new ways of improving their working lives: by moving departments, finding alternative projects and new friends and allies. All this happened in the 'shadow side' of the organization – unknown to, and unsanctioned by, the most senior managers.

must change from time to time, and there are clear indicators here that this company needs to learn how to do that in this respect. The problem is that if the directors are ignorant of what is going on, how can they learn from it? Creating the relationship with the leadership of any system as part of the structure of welcome for action learning is a key task for the accoucheur. The possibilities for organizational change and learning are greatly enhanced if the senior managers are engaged from the outset; yet, this can be one of the toughest parts of the job (Box 3.2).

Box 3.2 Casey on contracting

David Casey was a wise practitioner of action learning who took great pains to start on the right foot. In one instance he talks about pulling out of a starter workshop with the senior team, very late in the day:

> After much thought and at the last minute of the eleventh hour I refused to run the workshop. In the flurry of alarm and excitement generated by my decision, it became very clear that the chief executive had been pulling the wool over my eyes – he had no intention of undertaking a serious joint investigation with his colleagues about how they did their work together.
>
> (Casey 1993: 33)

In a second and very different case, he recounts how he had to persist with a critical question which proved very frustrating for the client but which eventually led to a significant breakthrough:

> In one organization I got on their nerves by persistently asking the question 'What is this group for?' over a period of nearly eight months. In exasperation two members of the group put their heads together and came up with four quite clear and largely separate purposes ... [which] ... led quickly to a complete rehash of their entire schedule of meetings.
>
> (Casey 1993: 50)

Casey was stubborn about getting his questions answered because he knew that, if there is ignorance of what action learning entails and if the quality of welcome is poor at the top, then there is unlikely to be much wider learning and little long-term innovation in that organization.

Action learning is no 'magic bullet'. It works best when it is well understood by its sponsors and when it is integrated into their strategic agenda. In the Hyundai Oilbank case (Box 3.3) the company was under severe pressure to change because of both internal and environmental factors.

Box 3.3 Case example: Hyundai Oilbank

Hyundai (hereafter) was hitting its lowest point in the years 2000 and 2001 due to its high cost business structure, unpredictable employment condition, and continued bad reputation as well as unfavorable external management environments such as being open to overseas markets and fierce competition in domestic markets. As a result, the company faced the worst financials of 451.7 million U.S. dollars in debts which led to the skyrocketing fall of shareholders' and external trust. In order to attack these fundamental problems in 2002, action learning was introduced as an innovative management tool for changing the way they work. A major reason why action learning was chosen was that the then CEO (recently retired in August, 2010) had had experience in action learning in a U.S. financial institution in his formative years.

Hyundai's action learning was initiated by the top management but in later years employees' team activities were brought up to the center in order to accomplish the 'Vision 2012' aimed at making them for 'the most effective oil refinery and marketing company in South Korea'. The company is using a coined word, *Let's* (Learning by Executing Together for Solutions), which is a new brand name for action learning since 2006. Action learning in the company has undertaken approximately 100 to 150 teams and four projects per year, and 2,000 projects total until 2009 from its inception, and delivered profits of 250 million U.S. dollars. As for compensation, the company throws an annual action learning conference to reward and share best practices, while three percent of financial gains (up to 50,000 U.S. dollars) are given to teams with outstanding performance.

In order to detail how to make action learning more explicit, the company produced a handbook for *Let's* participants to speak the same language in the problem-solving process. The contents of the *Let's* handbook include: the company's own definition and purpose of action learning, the *Let's* process, project selection, tools for problem-solving process (e.g., SWOT Analysis). Using ceremonies for project selection, sponsors and learning teams reach consensus on output images of an action learning project while sponsors make it clear what they want to get from the project. In addition, team leaders are mandated to become a learning coach so that they can enhance facilitative leadership in the team.

As a result of these orchestrated efforts, *Hyundai* was ranked the number one energy company on customer satisfaction in 2007 and, more importantly, the company has hugely improved its management performance from 2002 to 2009 including: (1) their credit rating has been enhanced from BBB to A0, (2) debts have decreased from 430% to 186%, and (3) accumulated profits have increased to 1.68 billion U.S. dollars. The head of the Performance Enhancement Team aptly witnessed, 'All of these performance indexes may not be the results of action learning only. Organizational employees, however, could improve problem-solving skills, collaboratively worked with other divisions, precisely spotted customer needs, and swiftly responded to competitors' moves through action learning.'

Source: Used with permission from Cho and Bong (2011)

Designing action learning

The objectives of senior management are obviously a major influence on any design for action learning. Once the strategy has been understood and the level of support assessed, there are various design issues to consider.

- introductory or preparatory workshops;
- recruiting set members – people willing to 'have a go' and who are open to learning;
- forming sets with *regular members* which focus on members' *problems or tasks* – supporting action, reflection and learning;
- recruiting clients with problems, challenges or opportunities with which they want help;
- finding sponsors who support set members in tackling these problems, challenges or opportunities and who help with accountability and evaluation of outcomes;
- choosing and developing action learning advisers or facilitators;
- holding conferences to link the sets with the whole project;
- evaluation.

How each of these happens – or whether it happens at all – depends upon the scale and sophistication of the action learning initiative. However, they are all questions which the action learning adviser as accoucheur can expect to be asked. This list, which is by no means exhaustive, shows how considerable the element of design is in the initiation role. There are many resources available on these design elements, on the web and in various workbooks – see for example Pedler (2003), Edmonstone (2003) and McGill and Brockbank (2004). In this account we focus on the more strategic aspects of design and in particular raise awareness of the way action learning is crafted to fit particular situations and contexts.

Who should be the set members?

This is an important question. Sometimes members are drawn from a particular strata, grade or profession; sometimes they are deliberately mixed across professions, departments or units; sometimes there is an open choice – anyone who wants to join and give it a go.

A key design parameter is: is there enough diversity of participants to give rise to fresh questions? This is a matter of judgement. There are many sources of diversity amongst people to be considered in any action learning design. As seen in the John Tann case in the previous chapter, managers from the same company, all similar in their personal characteristics: male, middle-aged, white etc., might provide enough diversity if they come, for example, from different locations. Some of Revans' early experiments with action learning involved colliery managers and deputies from adjacent mines meeting together to discuss productivity levels, accident rates and maintenance issue with each other (1982: 39–55). On the other hand, Revans also conducted projects in hospitals, where the full range of staff, including doctors, porters, auxiliaries, nurses and managers met together under action learning 'rules', e.g. equality of voice, listening to all etc. Such diverse sets worked on problems such as length of stay rates for particular illnesses, infection control and the training of student nurses (1982: 250–86).

As well as diversity, there is a need for commonality. Suitable participants may include people who share a responsibility for introducing new ideas or systems, who are experiencing or handling organizational restructurings or whose jobs share a high level of complexity especially in terms of relationships with customers, suppliers, communities, government departments etc. Other obvious sources of commonality are new starters, mid-career (and possibly stuck) professionals, anyone needing to innovate or learn something new, and anyone experiencing turbulence and ambiguity in their work. What is common about these situations is that they tend to be those in which people are open to learning; the diversity comes from the varying situations, contrasting personalities and differing life experiences.

The voluntary principle

Whatever their predicament or challenge, it is important that any participant should want to improve the situation they find themselves in. This is the most important aspect of commonality. Action learning needs willing participants with issues that they wish to tackle, and when this condition is met it means that all present are there as volunteers.

No one can be instructed to join in action learning. They can be commanded to present themselves at a certain time and place, but this is not at all the same thing. Any 'invitation' to take part in action learning should be accompanied by an escape route, to which a person who does not feel ready or who is already overburdened can have recourse without loss of dignity or approval.

This principle cannot be overstressed; it is the first and most vital. Learning (and action of the sort intended in action learning) are voluntary efforts that can only be undertaken and achieved through free will. If there are any 'pressed men' present this will soon be revealed, probably to the loss of all those concerned.

How should be challenges and problems be selected?

Problems and puzzles

Action learning is not for puzzles but for problems. Some people like to use the word 'challenge' or 'opportunity' instead of problem, which they see as being negative, or at least not positive enough. This does not matter – whatever works in the particular setting is fine – but what Revans signifies by the word problem is the situation for which there is as yet no known solution or obvious way forward. In other words, it is problematic.

Filling out a tax return, creating a school timetable or even building a new school may be experienced as problems but they are actually all *puzzles* in Revans' terminology. They all have right answers, and there are experts who can provide them. On the other hand, motivating a disaffected staff member, building a business or getting the most out of a merger, are all *problems* – there are no right answers. Though many books may claim the contrary and though there may be many who claim expertise, these are all problematic situations in which the best guarantee is careful experiment and learning.

Revans (1982: 716) made his own suggestions for the choosing of suitable problems:

A manager may study some changing aspect of:

i   A familiar task in a familiar setting
ii A familiar task in an unfamiliar setting
iii An unfamiliar task in a familiar setting
iv An unfamiliar task in an unfamiliar setting

This prescription has often been presented as in Figure 3.2. It might be argued that the effort and power of action learning is not really needed for 'own job' situations, which might not move people out of their comfort zones. If people are to choose problems or opportunities from this box, then that might call for some scrutiny, perhaps by fellow set members, to see whether there is enough challenge in what is being proposed. A good reason for choosing such a project would be if that person has not been doing this part of the job, for whatever reason, and now wishes to try.

These options are based on Revans' own experience where managers were sometimes seconded and exchanged between units or organizations and asked to tackle projects outside their areas of expertise. This creates a high degree of challenge but it is demanding to organize. It is again a question of what is possible in a particular situation; multi-organizational sets as in Figure 3.2 below, where projects are defined to require exposure to different perspectives in order to progress them, allow for some thinking outside one's own corporate experience without the requirement to actually go and conduct a project in another organization.

	Familiar TASK	*Unfamiliar* TASK
Familiar SITUATION	OWN JOB ISSUES	NEW JOB OR EXCHANGE PROJECT
Unfamiliar SITUATION	SAME JOB IN DIFFERENT SETTING	NEW PROJECT IN DIFFERENT UNIT/ORG.

Figure 3.2   Some options for challenges and problems

Do an organization survey?

One way to arrive at problems or challenges is to collect a list of issues in the organization or department. These can be collected by interviewing people in the department or unit concerned and asking them questions, such as:

- What opportunities do you see for improving what we do here?
- What goes wrong here and why do you think this is?
- If you could change one thing around here, what would it be?

It does not take long talking to a small but representative sample of people to come up with a list of potential issues for action learning. One such survey in a printing company produced a list from which the various set chose their issues for action and learning (see Box 3.4).

Box 3.4 Case example: Tomlinsons

Tomlinsons, a specialist printer, had various striking characteristics. Despite being very profitable, it had no managers, no trade unions and a flat but high wage rate for all employees irrespective of their varying skill levels and experience.

Like many small companies, the firm took its unusual character from the views of its owner and managing director, Mike Tomlinson. The vision and values for his own company came about as a consequence of his previous experience as the managing director of a much bigger printing concern. Here he had felt that managers and trade unions had been jointly responsible for the complex and convoluted wages system and for many of his other problems. His view was that it was better to pay people well, to have no designated managers, but to expect everyone to play a part in managing the plant.

Despite its high level of success, Tomlinsons had various issues and problems to be resolved, some of them as a result of these company policies. For example, if Mike was not around there were obvious difficulties in decision making. As the main contact with customers he was often out of the plant. Some of these gaps would be filled in an informal way by various people who would otherwise have been obvious candidates for supervisory and managerial roles.

As part of an Investors in People initiative facilitated by outside consultants, it was agreed that all 60 staff be offered the opportunity of being involved in action learning groups. The consultants spent two days talking to everyone in the plant and collecting issues for action. This resulted in a list of about 30 issues, problems and opportunities, including:

- computerization of the cutting list;
- redesign of job card;
- plan and supervision of new storage facility;
- redesign of a work process;
- improve relationships between work stations;
- strengthen relationships with customers;
- improve decision making;
- reduce waste of materials and improve recycling;
- reduce energy use;
- create a training programme for engravers.

One purpose of the programme was to promote an awareness of the whole system in which they were working, and to include the customers with whom most people had very limited contact. Sets were therefore formed by mixing staff from the eight different work stations in groups of four or five. Despite its size and the relatively simple flow process from design and initiation of film through cutting and engraving to despatch, many employees had little idea in detail of what their colleagues did.

Each set picked a joint problem from a list. Once they had chosen an issue, they had to get sign off from Mike Tomlinson, who also gave them some guidelines and his success criteria for the particular task. They had two hours per week of the firm's time over three months to work on these issues. Each set started with a training workshop on 'How to work as an effective group', but otherwise worked in a self-managed way without external facilitation (although one of the consultants made almost daily visits to the plant and did much informal coaching of teams).

As necessary, each set could meet with Mike Tomlinson to make proposals for action, which, if approved were then given back to the set to implement. In fact, Mike Tomlinson eventually approved all proposals but one, although it was not unusual for them to be sent back first for re-working. This was a crucial element which could not be faked or avoided, on either side.

At the end of the three months the firm was shut for the day and the staff convened in a local hotel where each set reported on (i) their actions and (ii) their learning. At the end of that day, Mike Tomlinson hosted a celebration dinner and thanked people for their efforts. Over the three months, many of the issues had been resolved or moved on. Of the 13 sets, 10 or 11 were judged by the consultants to have worked as planned in terms of successful action on tasks and learning from the process.

The Tomlinson case illustrates a situation well known to consultants: the problems and opportunities in the firm are well known – but not necessarily to senior managers. The difference in the action learning approach is that the insights gained from talking to staff around the organization are given back to them for investigation and action – and do not just adorn a consultancy report presented to the top team.

In talking about both the origins of action learning problems and the supportive assemblies needed to progress them, Revans talks about the importance of bringing together those who *know* about the problem; those who have the power or those who *can* do something about it with those who want to do something about because they *care* about it. As he says:

> . . . faced with the need to change a complex system of which the dynamics and the inertias are imperfectly understood, it is prudent . . . to consult those involved . . . the key people both supporting and acting upon the trial decisions, or opposing or resisting them, and it is these who must be assembled.
>
> (1971: 84–5)

An action learning programme

The ultimate aim for the accoucheur as the designer of any action learning programme is to establish the basis for the development of a learning community of the system in which the sets are working. This learning network will help the sets with their actions as seen above, but is even more important for the purpose of organizational learning, which is the focus of Chapter 5. This is often done by combining the small group work of the sets with larger conferences to bring people together to share learning and grasp the wider picture. In a study of organizational learning in a health authority (Nicolini et al. 2004), this principle is described as:

Sets = 'structures that reflect'
Conferences = 'structures that connect'

Sets are principally concerned with their own members and their goals, and there is a tendency for them to become rather inner focused, with little interest in the wider picture. A good programme design can help here by enabling sets to grasp the significance of their relationships with the whole system and become better connected. In one discussion of the learning community idea, Revans estimates that the 21 managers in his Belgian Inter-University Programme influenced over 200 other managers in the participating enterprises (1971: 81–2).

If there is only one action learning set, then they are the programme and must be encouraged to make their own connections with those who *know, care* and *can*. But if there are two sets or more then the accoucheur as designer can build in meetings to share what has been done and learned. Bringing several sets together can produce some inter-group rivalry, and again this can be part of the fun as long as it does not interfere with the learning. At these meetings, if it seems appropriate, sponsors and clients can also join in, although they must come in these roles and not as the people in charge. If there are a number of different organizations participating in the programme then bringing representatives from these enterprises together with the action learners is another possible move.

Obviously, the right form for an action learning programme depends on the situation, and upon who is involved and what their purposes are. Programmes can be entirely internal to the organization, as in the Tomlinson case, or they can be done in consortia or partnerships. Any organizations seeking to develop networked ways of working with one another may find that appropriately action learning sets are a good way to practise collaborative working. All this said, action learning programmes tend to have a number of similar components:

- *sets* of participants meeting every few weeks, over months and even years;
- often with a *set adviser* or *facilitator* – although they can meet successfully without them, in self-managed action learning mode (SMAL) as in the Tomlinson case above;
- *clients* and *sponsors*, the former to pose problems and opportunities, set expectations and success criteria; the latter to be a source of support, guidance, advice and perhaps some facilitation of action in a particular setting. Clients and sponsors can be the first port of call for reporting back findings and to help with evaluation;

- *face-to-face conferences* to start up programmes, to share learning at various points, to be part of evaluation and to celebrate successes. Conferences are opportunities for linking action learning sets with each other and with the wider 'learning community' in the organization or network of organizations concerned;
- *electronic networks* for up-to-the-minute reporting and connecting on issues. Sets can maintain contact with one another, store information and make decisions through private pages on a website. Organization-wide bulletin boards can be used to post matters of interest to all concerned. One multi-organizational community project agreed at the outset that each set would post a monthly report of actions and also questions – so that other sets could be involved in their work and influence each other's thinking.

The structure of the action learning programme in Figure 3.3 comes from a pharmaceutical company, where a major reorganization of the R&D division had recently taken place. This had created new teams, and the new team leaders took part in this programme with the help of external advisers. The problems addressed by the team leaders were essentially the same: *'How do we make this new job/team/structure work?'* Each leader was responsible for taking action on this challenge as it was manifest in their own patch, and it was also made clear from the outset that they had a

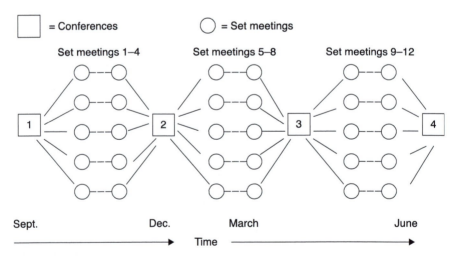

Figure 3.3   Structure of an action learning programme in a pharmaceutical R&D division

wider responsibility for making known any new understandings at the divisional company level.

The eight action learning sets of team leaders came together in three conferences over ten months. The start-up conference featured the CEO and Chairman of the parent company, who presented what they hoped would be achieved and promised to take a personal interest in the progress of the initiative. They also returned to the final conference to hear evaluation reports and join for dinner.

Following the formal end of the programme, half the sets continued to meet without external facilitators whilst selected streams of work were taken up for further development by project groups.

Planning for emergence

The term 'action learning programme' can be misleading, because it implies an ordered and predictable sequence of events. Action learning rarely works in this way and tends to be emergent, with new priorities developing over time. It is a mistake to try and specify every last component and pin down every last detail so that all spontaneous life is extinguished. The aim of the programme designer is to achieve a minimum critical specification, that is, the minimum – not the maximum – of structure, rules and procedures needed to make the collaboration work.

A programme like the one depicted in Figure 3.3 is likely to raise a number of issues and conflicts. These may range from questions about the logic of the new structure to arguments about the priorities of senior managers to suggestions for new initiatives. The appearance and voicing of these issues and conflicts may well be an indicator that the programme is working well. These questions, suggestions and disruptions are potentially the basis for new ways of working, so they are to be hoped for and expected, and need to be handled well when they emerge.

Examples of handling them badly include ignoring them, ridiculing them, suppressing them and protecting the boss from them. As this may be a kneejerk reaction for some managers, it is important to predict this possibility and to plan for it. This is also a key role for the accoucheur as designer, but it also the crossover point where the adviser moves from an initiation to an organizational learning role as in Chapter 5. This is a prompt to share the programme design and maintenance role with a wider group.

Action learning programmes should be part of a sequence of other activities for planning and learning in the organization. Any organization aspiring to be a learning company will have a regular cycle which looks at learning strategically in the context of planning future goals and direction. These ideas for 'learning architectures' are taken further in Chapter 5.

Evaluating action learning

> *The greatest danger is not that our aspirations are too high and we miss them; but that they are too low and we meet them.*
>
> Attributed to Michelangelo

Evaluation is a critical activity and should be planned in from the outset. Data from evaluation is a prime source for learning, and one rule of thumb is that you should devote 10 per cent of your time and resources to this activity. Whole books are written on evaluation and that is not part of our purpose here, although activities for evaluation can be found in various chapters of this book. For example, *The Organisational Readiness Questionnaire* here used as a pre-measure can also serve as a post-measure. the set meeting review sheet in Chapter 4 is a means of checking progress in the set and various ways of assessing learning at the organizational level are discussed in Chapter 5.

To evaluate something means to place a value upon it. Easy enough to say, but frequently hard to do. It is easier to assess learning in individuals and in the set than to measure the wider impact. What is the organizational benefit of the action and learning that happened in these sets? How can we know that this departmental or organizational shift came about through the actions of this group? There are so many intervening variables, so much else going on, that calculations such as these must usually be either left to consensus or be matters of speculation.

Yet, in parallel with this difficulty in assessing systemic outcomes, sponsors will often have big aspirations for action learning:

- 'I want people to ask for less permission and to take more initiative and risks.'
- 'How can we compete with lower-wage competitors? Only by shifting up, only by developing more of a culture of innovation.'
- 'We have lost the public service ethic that is so important to us, we must regain that, or re-invent it.'

And even

- 'I don't know, I just know we need something new . . . surprise me!'

Good evaluation need not be elaborate, but it can be a struggle to keep it simple and efficient. Aside from any technical difficulties as discussed above, this is because evaluation is also a political activity. Evaluation is about making judgements which are value based and involve fine distinctions between good and bad, better and worse. These judgements change depending on where you stand. Not everything is intensely political, but all organizing situations are political to some degree.

One response to this is to adopt a stakeholder approach to evaluation and ask all the interested parties what they want. This is good practice in many action learning situations. It means asking people for theircriteria for measuring value: what are your 'success criteria'? The simple outline in Box 3.5 can be used – with suitable adjustments to the wording – with individual action learners, sets, sponsors, clients or senior teams.

Box 3.5 Success criteria for action learning

Looking at the situation which the action learning is intended to improve . . .

1   How would you recognize progress? How will you know when the situation has changed? (Be as specific as possible.)

2   Who are the main stakeholders in this situation? How would each of them recognize progress?

(i)

(ii)

(iii)

etc.

3   What do you think will be learned as a result of tackling this situation?

Having said something about the difficulties, it needs to be emphasized that evaluation is both a necessary and vital activity in action learning. Improving the ability to self-evaluate is a key aspect of critical thinking (see Chapter 6) and an important learning outcome in itself. It is a mark of maturity when people, groups and organizations evaluate their own actions and learning. Carrying out a more formal evaluation, for example, by interviewing stakeholders and assessing how far their expectations have been met, can be a good task for an action learning set to do together. As a collective review of their work and learning it can be an excellent way to 'make a good end'.

A simple matrix (see Figure 3.4) can be used to collect success criteria from all the stakeholders to an action learning process and this forms in turn a basis for evaluation. Telephone conversations or interviews with those concerned can be used to fill out the matrix, which then becomes a useful aid to learning and future direction.

The adviser as accoucheur does not necessarily conduct the evaluation themselves, but they will have an important say in its design. Evaluation is an activity which every action learner should do as part of their efforts at action learning. In some circumstances specialists might also be engaged to provide an external view.

Before moving on to the next chapter on set advising, make some practice notes on your approach to the accoucheur role.

Stakeholder	Success criteria	Evidence needed
1 Customer		
2 Manager		
3 Team Y		
etc.		

Figure 3.4   A stakeholder evaluation matrix

My practice notes 3

The accoucheur

Make some notes on each aspect of the action learning adviser's role as it relates to your current practice. You may want to consider such questions as:

- Is this a part of what I do now? Should it be?

- Which aspect of the accoucheur and designer role appeals to me most?

- Which aspects do I find more difficult or questionable?

- What are my priorities for development in these aspects?

Considering the idea of organizational readiness

Gaining support and commitment from the top

Designing action learning including recruiting set members and problems/opportunities

Designing action learning programmes

Evaluation

Reflection on *My practice notes 3*:
Reading through what I have just written on these aspects of the accoucheur/designer role, what does it say about me and my practice?

Deller Business Services

A case study in advising on action learning

Introduction

Deller Business Services is a case study in three parts. These parts follow on from one another and appear successively at the end of Chapters 3, 4 and 5.

The case depicts an action learning intervention in a large enterprise and simulates the three roles of the action learning adviser – accoucheur, set adviser and developer of organizational learning. The purpose of the case is to bring this model to life and to help you reflect on your own practice in these roles.

The case is based on an actual one, but includes data drawn from a number of projects. In each part you are invited to look at the information given and decide how you would act in the situation. You can then find details of what happened next at the end of the following chapter, where you will also be invited to respond again. Obviously, there are no right answers!

Background

Deller Business Services provides managerial and outsourcing services to companies, public agencies and government-regulated industries. It began as a private sector provider which, in 2008, acquired LGC, a company specializing in offering outsourced services to local government, since when it has expanded considerably into the public sector.

Much of the company's work is in the UK but it has worldwide contracts, including in Ireland, China and Australasia. In this highly competitive business environment, Deller was awarded 'Top 20 Best Big Company to Work For' status in *The Sunday Times* rankings in 2008 and also achieved

Three Star accreditation for an 'outstanding level of employee engagement' from *Best Companies*.

LGC was set up as a business in 1997 to provide outsourced services including information technology, building maintenance, estate management, traffic and transport planning and business processes (pensions, payroll, human resources and training). At that time LGC consisted mainly of staff transferred in from the councils where it held contracts, and it operated in a very similar way to the previous set-ups, retaining many of the structures and with a predominantly local government culture.

Six months before the action learning programme was proposed LGC was closed down when it was acquired by Deller Business Services, and all the staff were transferred to the new organization.

* * *

Deller Business Services

A case study in advising on action learning

PART 1

Part 1 – Design

The Head of Organizational Development for Deller Business Services sends you the following email:

Dear Chris

Thank you for agreeing to present a proposal for an action learning programme to support our managers through a period of transition for the organization.

As you know, Deller Business Services has recently acquired a new company to add to our portfolio to supply outsourced services to the public sector.

This acquisition is populated by highly specialized areas of finance, property, human resources, information technology and business and people services. Many are typified by chartered and professional qualifications and specialized knowledge. A silo based approach to the organizational structure has dominated for many years. In the past there has been little attention given to developing management thinking, leadership and collaborative working.

As a result of the acquisition we have now established a new team of six senior directors, drawn equally from the acquired company and parent company. The 60 managers who work to this team have all retained their previous posts.

The programme we wish to commission should be a process of business improvement which:

- *creates a paradigm shift in management thinking and reflection;*
- *promotes joint working/collaboration/partnership thinking;*
- *provides a highly cost effective process for continuing (and enduring) management development and self-managed learning;*
- *encourages innovation and prompts creative solutions for business problems;*
- *challenges and stimulates our people, and nurtures competitive thinking;*
- *facilitates the sharing of knowledge, experience and ideas;*
- *accelerates organizational and personal learning;*
- *is real work related and action focused.*

The Directors were impressed by your presentation on action learning and we would like to hear further your thoughts on a design for a programme that supports our objectives.

On behalf of the Executive Team we look forward to meeting you and hearing your proposal on Wednesday.

Kind regards

Mike

*   *   *

Task 1

Using ideas from Chapter 3, your task is to propose a design for an action learning programme for Deller Business Services to present at your meeting with the Executive Team.
   Make some notes on:

(i)   Likely features of the design, and the design elements that need to be addressed:

(ii)   Further questions you need to ask before your presentation

(You will find a response to this task at the end of the next chapter.)

4　The set adviser

Chapter overview

The set adviser or facilitator is the most familiar role taken by action learning practitioners. Despite Revans' concerns, most action learning sets employ such 'supernumaries' (as he called them). We use the term 'set adviser' in preference to 'set facilitator', although this is the term is most commonly used. We do this in order to emphasize the nature of the role as envisaged by Revans as advisory to the set. It is not an executive role and the adviser should beware of exercising too much influence and avoid taking too much of a lead. To take a dominant role is to take away the autonomy of the set, and make it less likely that it will mature to self-direction. The success of the set adviser comes when the set no longer needs their help – because they can do it themselves.

The set adviser can play an important part in helping others to become more effective in terms of their actions, reflection, learning and ability to self-facilitate. To encourage set members to develop the skills of presenting issues, listening, questioning, reflecting and acting requires facilitative leadership (Chapter 7) in keeping the focus on the set and helping members to support and challenge each other. Many set advisers aim for a gradual withdrawal from the set as the members grow in confidence and take on the facilitation functions for themselves.

This chapter also includes a section on virtual action learning (VAL), which perhaps deserves a chapter to itself. VAL is an important new development in action learning, with new skill requirements and offering new opportunities, not only for action learning but also for the wider practices of organizing and leadership. This chapter concludes with the second part of Deller Business Services *which appears at the end of Chapters 3, 4 and 5. The Deller case depicts an action learning intervention in a large enterprise, and you are invited to test your knowledge and skills in the action learning adviser's role as the case develops.*

This chapter contains:

- Introduction
- Pre-set preparation

- Creating space for the set meeting

- Ground rules

- Meeting process

- Focus: how action learning differs

- Support and challenge

- Questioning

- Reflecting, reviewing, recording

- Ending

- Virtual action learning

- My practice notes 4

- Case study: Deller Business Services – Part 2

Introduction

In Chapter 2, we noted how Revans was concerned to limit the role of set advisers, describing them as supernumeraries or 'combiners' needed only to help sets get started. Although he consistently warned against the dangers of undue influence from this 'non-involved facilitator' (Revans 2011: 10), surveys suggest that most action learning sets do have advisers or facilitators (Pedler et al. 2005), and some writers now see the role as central.

Various reasons are cited for this; set advisers are needed because of:

- a lack of understanding amongst set members about the process of action learning;
- a need for help or set members to get to know each other;
- a need for someone who is responsible for helping the group in their action and learning;
- the lack of skills for set members to facilitate themselves;
- the expectations of participants or sponsors.

There is perhaps now a general agreement amongst writers since Revans that good facilitation helps in creating successful action learning sets. The set adviser encourages the asking of questions and the sharing of information and ideas; helps make learning explicit; and helps deal with conflicts. This developed view of the set adviser role overlaps with, and also contrasts with, the general facilitator of groups, who usually takes a stronger lead in

Casey (2011)	Edmonstone (2003)	O'Hara et al. (2004)	Weaver and Farrell (1997)	Heron (1999)
SET ADVISERS	SET ADVISERS	SET ADVISERS	FACILITATORS	FACILITATORS
• Facilitate giving • Facilitate receiving • To clarify the various processes of action learning • To help others take over tasks 1, 2 and 3	• Reading self • Reading the set • Sense making for the group • Nudging or interventions, e.g. acting as role model, encouraging membership, ensuring the environment is good, encouraging participation, managing time, enabling learning by questions and reflections	• Questioning skills • Active listening skills • Ability to give and receive feedback • Understanding of group processes • Creative problem-solving skills • Skill of reflection • Understanding the process of learning	• Task – the work the group do • Process – actions and processes that help the group to get the work done • Group – understanding • Self awareness and understanding	• Planning – goal oriented • Meaning – found in group and individual experience • Confronting – raising consciousness about resistance • Feeling – management of emotion • Structuring – of the learning • Valuing – maintaining integrity and respect

Figure 4.1   Some views on the roles of the set adviser and the group facilitator

setting goals and prescribing processes. Figure 4.1 shows the views of three action learning writers (Edmonstone 2003; O'Hara et al. 2004; Casey 2011) alongside two writers (Weaver and Farrell 1997; Heron 1999) on general facilitation.

Action learning advisers share many skills with more general facilitators, for example: 'Effective facilitators understand and encourage improvement of group dynamics. They know how to use their presence to help a group accomplish its task and become more productive' (Wilson 2010: 292). Yet, there are important differences: in action learning the adviser helps the set to become a powerful system for action and learning, via 'questioning insight' and the developing potential for learning, reflection and problem solving (Lowe 2010: 85–7; Wilson 2010).

A study of an action learning programme for NHS leaders reveals a large number of ways in which set advisers can add value by example and practice (Pedler and Abbott 2008 – all quotes are from set participants)

1   *Personal conviction and commitment to action learning*

Advisers have to be carefully selected – there is a difference between facilitation and training. They have to be very confident and really believe in action learning. This adviser had not really bought into action learning, I don't think they knew how to manage the process and to steer a diverse group on action learning.

People felt very confused and wanted to be given a task (but, in a previous set with a strong adviser) . . . he would have said 'make a strong steer and task for yourself'.

2   *Sense of purpose*

The adviser was very clear in terms of purpose . . . that purposefulness drove us on through difficult times.

When things are difficult, as they were last year in the NHS, many people in the set did not even know if they would have jobs to go to, it is very difficult to take a day out of work. Without a sense of purpose and no clarity around the task we could not go on. [The adviser] quickly instilled a sense of purpose and vibrancy.

3   *Structure and discipline*

We had the structure of describing what happened from the actions of the last meeting; being clear about the evidence from what happened; discussing the impact of what happened; then exploring the alternative courses of action.

. . . was from the independent sector, he was very powerful and very committed to action learning, he knew how to use the language. . . . He said things like 'How do you want to handle the next session?' He always made it clear that it was our set, and he always made time for us personally.

4   *Support*

She listened to the problem discussions and helped us to think them through and crystalise our thoughts.

Showing that they really care about you and your project – that sounds a bit soppy but it mattered.

5   *Challenge*

She was a critical friend.

She also challenged us to challenge the opinionated person more. She felt that we were a bit 'fluffy'. We did challenge but in a nice supportive way. Most of us were nurses by profession, all caring people. I think some members of the group did become more challenging.

6   *Feedback*

It's like a one way mirror in that as participants we describe an experience and others give feedback on what they see and hear and reflect that back to you. Behind the mirror the adviser helps you to feed back and make sense of what is happening on the other side of the mirror, what I am thinking, feeling, what I want.

We were encouraged to describe the situation then self-appraise it, and articulate the outcome we wanted. The group fed back what they had heard and we then individually agreed learning points.

7   *Encouragement to action*

Encouraging us to take action for ourselves. The set definitely influenced the actions I took, especially through the reflection time away from everyday practice – you think on the way to meetings and on the way back – you think: 'Hmmn, I might try that.'

8   *Self-awareness*

Our adviser was very aware of her own preferences and filters. This self-awareness so openly exhibited was an education in itself.

9   *Learning about learning*

I learned a new way of learning. I was sceptical at the beginning. I thought this is just talking for the day – we met in a beautiful place and often went for a walk – it felt indulgent! The adviser was crucial in making it happen – not just a talking shop but a learning experience. I am now far more likely to meet up with a colleague for coffee or go out for a walk to discuss action without thinking it's a waste of time – I have become more purposeful in my conversations.

10 *Accountability to the set*

Our adviser gave the strong impression that it was the group he was accountable to. He was more of a participant in that he asked others for feedback on the process, and explored his own impact on others.

Pre-set preparation

There are a number of important matters that must be dealt with before any set meets, most of which have been dealt with in Chapter 3. However, there are practical and logistic aspects to preparing for meetings, including:

- arranging and checking the venue;

- access for the less able;
- transport and/or parking facilities;
- arranging refreshments;
- checking the times of the meeting;
- contacting set members with the arrangements.

These are often best done by set members, for the practical reason that they might have the best access to local resources, but also because taking on these 'housekeeping' tasks is a small but significant step towards self-management and self-facilitation. There are times when set advisers have to undertake this work, especially in the early stages, and there are aspects that cannot be delegated, for example contacting members before the meeting to encourage them to prepare themselves. The proforma in Box 4.1 is useful for this purpose.

Box 4.1 Action learning problem brief

These questions will help you to think through a suitable problem, opportunity or issue for action learning:

1   Describe your situation, problem or challenge in one sentence.

2   Why is this important?

(i)   To you?
(ii) To your organization?

3   How will you recognize progress on this problem?

4   Who else would like to see progress on this problem?

5   What difficulties do you anticipate?

6   What are the benefits if this problem is reduced or resolved:

(i)   to me?
(ii)   to other people?
(iii) to the organization?

Source: Adapted from Pedler (2008: 47–8)

Other essential preparation for the adviser includes reading notes from previous meetings (see below on Reflecting, reviewing, recording) (page 77) and readying oneself emotionally and psychologically. To be 'authentically present', or to show up in good order both mentally and physically, may involve particular activities such as meditation (Owen 1997; Caulat 2006). This is a matter of personal practice: one of us likes to arrive early at any venue, sit in each chair in turn and look at the shared space from each perspective.

Creating space for the set meeting

Creating a good environment for a learning set is essential. As Edmonstone notes (2003) the consequences of a poor environment or of not protecting the boundaries of the set can destroy the quality of space needed. One participant reports:

> We ended up using one member's office, which seemed like a good idea at the time . . . [but] . . . it may have been a false economy. We were at work after all . . . [and] . . . I couldn't switch into learning mode easily. The person whose office it was, was good about switching phones off, etc., but it didn't stop people wandering in with 'As you are here, could you look at this'. At breaks it was noticeable that we all rushed off to 'just photocopy', 'just make a telephone call', 'just sort xyz out'.
>
> (Pedler and Abbott 2008: 191–2)

Place and environment are keys parts of ensuring that the set becomes a 'communicative space' where 'people can bring their spirit as well as their mind to work' (Rigg in Mead 2006: 160). Without this quality of presence people are less able to undertake the 'emotional labour' of making sense of the tensions and the demands of their situations (Mead 2006: 159–61).

Ground rules

Ground rules are an action and learning contract agreed between the set members. They are ways of working together which enable the set to do their work well and that reflect action learning values.

Each set should create its own ground rules to shape the way they will work over the cycle of meetings. What do we need as rules to create a supportive but challenging learning environment? Here are some examples from sets we have been in (Figure 4.2):

Practical	Behavioural
• Attendance and punctuality • The duration of meetings and breaks • Declaration of conflicts of interest • Reviewing the ground rules • Note taking – who owns the notes and what happens to any notes taken • Each person to have equal voice and time • How the set celebrates achievement or their time together • The use of jargon	• Confidentiality • Commitment • Respect for and between each other • Non judgemental • Being responsible for self • Using I not we – 'so we all know that' becomes 'I know that' • Support and challenging each other • The right to say NO or to decline to respond to question or challenge

Figure 4.2 Some ground rules

Confidentiality often comes at the top of lists, and can usefully be tested by the set adviser: what, exactly, do we mean by confidentiality? For example: are people allowed to discuss what they learned outside this set? And if so, how, and with whom?

Asking these questions may highlight that what seems simple is not. In one case, a set member disclosed a fraud in the organization but claimed that the group had signed up to confidentiality and that they therefore must keep this to themselves. This caused great unease from which the set never entirely recovered. There is perhaps no ultimate protection against such cases, but by testing assumptions and the limits of what is taken for granted, the adviser can usefully help the set to develop a shared understanding of the meaning of each rule.

Ground rules should be considered as provisional and open to change. They can be revisited at any meeting to consider whether they are still relevant.

Meeting process

Though there is no fixed pattern and sets should create their own rhythms, a set meeting often includes these activities:

- *Catch-up* – a short round where members can share with each other the actions and developments since the previous meeting. This is a good way of starting because it serves to pull the set back together, but timekeeping can be difficult as catch-ups can easily run on. Sets operate with varying strictness on this, some even setting specific time limits.

- *Setting the meeting agenda* – including establishing a 'batting order' of turn taking; and while many sets have the ground rule of equal time for members, this may be modified by agreement here depending on the urgency of individual issues.
- *Turn-taking* – presenting challenges or problems and receiving questions and feedback (see 'Support and challenge' below). This tends to take up most of the meeting time and may follow the pattern of each member reporting on their progress since the previous meeting, describing the issue as they see it now, being offered questions and feedback from other set members (see 'Questioning' below), considering their options and committing to any actions they will take before the next meeting.
- *Learning review* – where members review their learning, individually and collectively as a set (see 'Reflecting and reviewing' below).

Focus: how action learning differs

Reflecting on the pattern and focus of communication is a useful thing for set advisers to do in the early stages. Once noticed, this awareness becomes second nature to set members. Whatever patterns of working are adopted by sets, there is a characteristic aspect of communication in action learning. Unlike in a *discussion group* where the rule is to follow the topic under discussion, the *action learning set* keeps its focus on the person and the problem (see Figure 4.3).

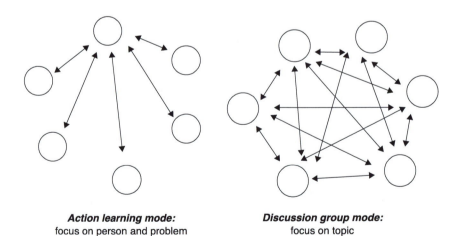

Action learning mode:
focus on person and problem

Discussion group mode:
focus on topic

Figure 4.3 Modes of discussion and action learning

The focus on the person (or persons) is really shorthand for saying *Person + Problem + Context* (Figure 4.4).

Figure 4.4 is a way of representing Revans' three systems of alpha, beta and gamma (1982: 625–51) as they appear in the 'communicative space' of the set. The power of the focus or gaze that action learning sets can develop spotlights the person (which can at times be hard or uncomfortable to hold), but also illuminates the problem and the context in which the action takes place.

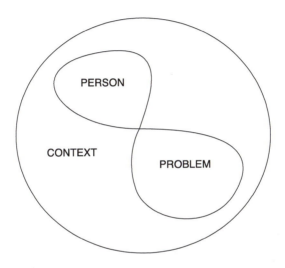

Figure 4.4   The system of person/problem/context

Support and challenge

Sets vary greatly in their effectiveness, both compared with one another and over time, and the set adviser can add value by encouraging members to aspire to what they cannot achieve without the set. A successful set, as judged by its members, clients and sponsors, requires a good balance of challenge and support. Ideally we want high support and high challenge at the same time (Figure 4.5).

A common error is to attempt too much challenge too early. Revans said that warmth comes before light, and to up the level of challenge in a set requires a higher level of support, from what he called 'comrades in adversity'.

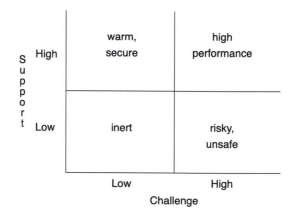

Figure 4.5 The balance of support and challenge

Nothing supports people more than being listened to; and nothing challenges more than a good question that makes you stop and think about what you are trying to do and why. Yet these are deceptively simple solutions; otherwise these opportunities would not be as rare as they are. A skilled adviser helps here, first, by being aware of the current levels of support and challenge as vital signs in any set, like blood pressure in the person. As an adviser, one of the first things you notice about a set is how warm or cold is it in here? Sharp or muddled? If these qualities are out of balance, the adviser can ask the group to score themselves on the two dimensions of Figure 4.5 and then ask them what they think about the consequences of the group climate and how it relates to their work.

Questioning

Questioning insight comes when new insight is gained through members being helped to question themselves and their situations, especially on that which they may not have previously considered. Revans' three questions (1982: 715) can be asked in relation to any situation:

- Who knows about (understands) this problem?
- Who cares about it?
- And who can do anything about it?

These connect with three central processes of human action: thinking, feeling and willing (Figure 4.6).

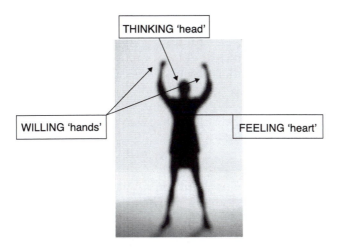

Figure 4.6   Thinking, feeling and willing

Thinking – about ideas, facts and theories – is traditionally thought of as being associated with the head, and is termed 'cognitive' by psychologists. Questions which explore thinking do so by looking for information, assumptions and alternatives. For example:

- Can you tell me more about this problem?
- What are your customers saying to you?
- What makes this problem so exciting/important/challenging?
- Who else is involved?
- Who has the power to make it happen?
- How important is it to them that this problem is resolved?
- Whose help do you need?
- Who has specialist knowledge?
- How do you interpret all that data?
- What sense are you making from the feedback you are receiving?
- Is there a pattern in the way this set meeting is going?

Feeling – about sensations, moods and emotions – is traditionally associated with the heart, and is termed 'affective' by psychologists. Questions which explore feeling do so by exploring feelings, responses, sympathies and intuitions. For example:

- Why is this so important to you?
- How did you feel when you heard that?
- If I was in that situation I would be angry – how about you?

- How do you feel about the questions you have been asked in this group?
- Who else cares about this situation?
- What do you think is blocking this situation?
- You say that the others would not be interested – where do their sympathies lie?
- What does your intuition tell you about the issue?
- How are you feeling right now?
- How would you like to feel about this?

Willing – intentions, movement and action is traditionally thought of as in the hands and feet and is termed 'conative' by psychologists. Questions which explore willing do so by exploring action, direction, planning and goals. For example:

- Can you describe how things will be in one, five and ten years' time?
- How will you decide what action to take?
- What help or support might you need?
- How will you get that support?
- What alternatives are there?
- What will you do next?
- If you plan is accepted how will you tell the team?
- What can you do to make sure this happens next time?
- You said last time that you were going to raise the issue with your manager, and you haven't!
- What shall we do at the next meeting?

In action learning there is also the fourth dimension of *learning*, which is an aspect that the set adviser will pay particular attention to. The purpose of the questioning about learning is to promote taking stock, reflecting, reviewing and evaluating:

- What have you achieved since the last meeting?
- What made this happen?
- What are the things you have learned from the experience?
- What have we achieved as a group?
- What has helped?
- What could we do more/less of?
- How could you create similar opportunities back at work?
- What conditions have helped us/you learn?
- How could we do things differently?

The adviser may often model such questions, especially the last set, in the interests of all members acquiring this valuable skill. The more able the members, the more likely they are to self-facilitate, with each taking this role in turn or carrying it out collectively. As David Casey (2011) puts it most succinctly (see Figure 4.1 above), the set adviser's role can be summed up in just four tasks: to facilitate giving, to facilitate receiving, to clarify the various processes of action learning *and to help others take over tasks 1, 2 and 3* (our emphasis).

Reflecting, reviewing, recording

In some occupations such as health and social care, reviewing one's practice, reflecting on it and recording learning points is a critical marker of professional development. Whilst less common in other parts of the vocational world, learning from practice so as to do better in the future is part of what it means to be a professional.

Marshall (2001) notes two arcs of attention in reflective enquiry, the inner and the outer. The inner arc focuses on assumptions, patterns of activity, our response to others, the language we use and the way we make sense of what is going on. The outer arc focuses on what is going on around us, how we are affecting others, how we are maintaining or changing a situation, how we test our assumptions and how others are making sense of the same event. Both arcs of attention can be useful to set members in reflecting on set meetings. This can be done by using a review sheet at the end of the meeting, to be quickly completed by each set member and shared with others, but also kept as a record and reviewed as preparation for subsequent meetings (Box 4.2).

An alternative approach adopts the 'Thinking/Feeling/Willing' model used earlier (Box 4.3, see page 81).

A learning diary is another means of developing the habit of reflection. This can be used both to record set meetings and to make connections with the workplace, although it requires self-discipline and commitment to work well. An alternative to the individual learning diary is for members to email each other with weekly reflections, perhaps on critical incidents at work.

In Chapter 8 we examine how set advisers can develop their own practice through self-reflection. As an adviser you probably take some notes to keep a basic record and perhaps for future reflection. This may include actions that set members have committed to, and actions you may need to take before the next meeting. A learning diary or log book might look like the one in Box 4.4 (see page 82).

Box 4.2 Set meeting review sheet

Spend five minutes reflecting individually on the work of the set and before sharing your thoughts with fellow members on:

1   **MY PROBLEM/CHALLENGE** The three key things I have learned about my issue today are:

(i)
(ii)
(iii)

2   **MYSELF** The one thing I've learned about myself today is:

3   **ACTION** My action steps before the next meeting are:

(i)
(ii)
etc.

4   **OTHER SET MEMBERS** The most interesting thing I have learned today about the problems facing each of the other set members is:

(i)
(ii)
(iii)
(iv)
(v)
etc.

5   **THE SET** The thing that stands out for me today in terms of the working of this set is:

Box 4.3 Set meeting review sheet — *Thinking/Feeling/Willing*

Spend five minutes reflecting individually on the work of the set and before sharing your thoughts with fellow members on:

Thinking – What do I now think about my problem or issue?	*Feeling* – How do I now feel about my problem or issue?	*Willing* – What do I now intend to do about my problem or issue?
Thinking – What do I think about the working of the set?	*Feeling* – How do I feel about the working of the set?	*Willing* – What do I intend to do more of or less of in this set?

One final point on any notes in action learning: are these seen as strictly personal? Or can they be read by others? Agreements on this can be included in the ground rules.

Ending

Making a good end is the last step in the set's work. Even where sets begin with a fixed lifetime in terms of the number of meetings, there is still the question, explicit or not, as to whether they will continue at the end of that time. Committing to a number of meetings at the outset, say four to six, creates a natural review point, and should facilitate discussion in which members can speak freely about what they want. If the set decides

Box 4.4 A log book

Date:

Place:

Present:

Summary of meeting:

Mark the scales below in terms of who did what at this meeting:

Climate: members	Adviser	. . . .	. .. . .	set
Questioning: members	Adviser	. . . .	. .. . .	set
Feedback: members	Adviser	. . . .	. .. . .	set
Support: members	Adviser	. . . .	. .. . .	set
Challenge: members	Adviser	. . . .	. .. . .	set

What can I do at the next set meeting to shift the responsibility more to the members?

When will the set be able to self-facilitate so that I can withdraw?

My actions for the next meeting:

(i)

(ii)

(iii)

etc.

to continue then this is an easy place for the adviser to withdraw and for the set to draw up a new contract.

Where sets make a conscious decision to finish, this is an important opportunity for a celebration. Acknowledging what has been achieved can take many forms; from a glass of wine to the exchange of gifts, to the lengthy evaluation process including stakeholders, with which one set concluded their two years of work. Making a good end to a period of productive life and work together, and marking the occasion appropriately, is a valuable accomplishment in itself.

Withdrawing before the set has ended is a trickier business for the set adviser, even when it has been previously stated as an intention. Though many practitioners of Revans' action learning hold it to be a mark of success to leave a set freestanding and self-facilitating, advisers also become friends. And there are other factors, such as Nancy Dixon's insight, quoted in Chapter 2, on the difficulty of relinquishing the attractive role of being 'wise and insightful'.

Whilst this process cannot be avoided, there are some things you can do as an adviser to make withdrawing easier: you can . . .

- maintain awareness of the dangers of too much dependency on you as the adviser, and share this with the set as appropriate;
- make it clear to the set the outset that you intend withdrawing – and if possible at what point in the programme;
- offer a fixed 'budget' of your time with the set, say four meetings if there is a committed to six, and let them fix which meetings these are (which also promotes self-facilitation);
- continuously recognize the development of membership and self-facilitation skills in set meetings;
- encourage members to take turns in facilitating each other in your presence and receive feedback;
- be aware of your own feelings about leaving the set, and make these public if appropriate; don't pretend it's easy.

Virtual action learning

This chapter has so far proceeded on the assumption that action learning sets meet face-to-face (f2f). A few years ago that sentence would have engendered a double-take, but virtual action learning (VAL) is now emerging as an important new practice for the set adviser. The era of virtual living and learning via emerging technologies is transforming human interaction. Some see this as so significant that they think that it is changing what it means to be human; we are becoming 'digital natives' who think differently: 'They develop hypertext minds. They leap around. It's as though their cognitive structures were parallel not sequential' (Winn in Shepherd 2011: 20).

VAL takes place in 'a virtual environment, rather than f2f, via a range of enabling, interactive and collaborative technologies' (Dickinson et al. 2010: 59), and is already an umbrella term, encompassing a number of alternative practices, with synchronous and asynchronous varieties:

- Synchronous varieties (real-time or simultaneous interaction) include instant messaging, webinars, audio and web-based conferencing. Here parties listen and respond to each other in real time, as though they are in the room together.
- Asynchronous varieties (delayed interaction) include podcasts, recorded messages and discussion boards, where questions or responses can be posted at any time within agreed timescales. This helps people working in widely different time zones or with atypical work patterns.

Box 4.5 gives a case example of VAL in a global transport company.

Box 4.5 VAL in a global transport company

A global transport company employed action learning as part of its senior management programme. Whilst seen as successful, the programme relied on managers arriving from all parts of the world for one week modules, where the action sets met on days 1 and 5 with a three day training workshop in between. This was expensive, tiring and time consuming and when the workshops went online as e-learning, it was an opportunity to try VAL.

> To be honest we thought it was a no-brainer – we would just do action learning through the company web meeting software. We didn't think there would be a problem and in fact managers would appreciate the flexibility not having to travel and we would save money and time. It didn't occur to us that this was not just a 'shade of the same colour but a new colour altogether'.

An external set adviser facilitated the action learning sets via the company system, supported by a discussion board. After the first year a website was created for the programme with a 'people wall' where photos and biographies were posted by set members. There was also a set meeting wall with a private area for each set where details of meetings, protocols and ground rules were posted, and a communication wall where sets could post anything they felt would be helpful to other sets.

A year after the end of the programme the action learning programme was evaluated and included the following comments from participants, the adviser and the sponsor:

Comments from participants:

Asynchronous

- It relied on a strong discipline to participate.

- I could contribute when and how I found appropriate – so from my computer, i-phone etc.

- I found it difficult to understand the tone of the 'conversation'. Culturally it was difficult, e.g. exclamation marks are aggressive in my culture whereas in another it marks humour.

- I was really careful about what I wrote – it would be there for ever and could be used out of context.

- As a reflective person I was really able to spend time thinking about a response.

Synchronous

- Easy to opt out or leave early – the signal could get lost when I got fed up!

- The quality of presence was not discussed.

- It was great not having to travel for a day activity.

- I liked the change of venue – leaving work behind – with this it was hard to get prepared because at my desk one minute I was working the next minute I was 'in'.

- The meeting relies on reliable technology – fine if you are in Europe or the States but Angola?

- Working in another language I could spend time getting the translation right.

- It was disciplined and the conversation more focused.

- It was easy to ignore someone!

- Being challenged was harder – I had no idea about the context in which I was asking the question.

- Face to face we met at each other's workplace and this meant we had a feeling for each other's work context – I missed this.

- Harder to opt out because there was a written record of participation.

- I was constantly looking at the forum for a reply to something I had posted – I found this very stressful.

- Easy to self-facilitate – i.e. each person opened the forum was holding the space.

- I found myself over-engineering questions and responses. In some ways this activity helped my questioning skills, on the other hand it was very time consuming.

- Time zone differences meant as the only person in the USA I was getting up in the early hours of the morning!

- It felt more focused.

- It was easier to self-facilitate.

- I could focus on listening rather than getting distracted by the visual.

- I didn't feel confident that it was not being recorded or that someone else was listening in and monitoring performance.

- I couldn't tell whether people` were really listening.

- It was difficult to remove myself from work – even if I just moved to the conference room I was still there.

- I don't speak good English and have a strong accent – I found it hard to understand others and be understood. f2f I could manage better.

- I liked the anonymity of the set – I could choose who I was – create a character and act it out.

Comments from the adviser:

- I found it hard to keep up with the discussion board, whereas I can book time out for a set meeting, discussion boards feel as though you have to be forever present (asynchronous).
- I found it hard when participants made derogatory remarks about the programme on the discussion board (asynchronous) – if it was f2f I could manage that – but in writing it hurt!
- I was definitely behind set members in using the technology (synchronous), because it was their organization's system we were using they were way ahead – so I often fumbled at the beginning and felt stupid as they got impatient with me.
- I found it really focused the meeting (synchronous).
- When we introduced a website with the various walls – it created the sense of community that was missing before and started to create a shared meaning for the activities in the set meeting.

Comments from the sponsor:

- There was no doubt it saved money from the training budget, but managers said that they could have justified the cost by doing other business at the headquarters, or that there was a richness of just being with others and again experiencing at a deeper level the headquarter environment.
- The groups didn't build the same affection for each other as the face-to-face groups who also ate together, drank together, went to a ball game etc. (the website in year two helped with this).
- The programme reflected the way we work – many meetings are now held through the internal webinar technology.
- Managers who had taken part in the VAL appeared to be more confident and skilled in virtual business meeting, both internally and externally – that's important because it's how we do business.

In this case, it is obvious that the 'actor network' of the interrelated people, processes and technologies that are created in VAL raises some new professional issues for the action learning adviser.

In Table 4.1 these are considered under the three headings of design, facilitation and organizational learning.

Online communication

It is suggested that the virtual environment needs different communication skills from both the adviser and set members (Caulat 2006; Caulat and De Haan 2006; Dickinson et al. 2010; Caulat 2012). Experienced advisers learn to read visual clues such as eye contact, but online communication requires protocols and other ways to sense the set, such as focusing exercises, interrupting and 'virtual nodding' (Caulat 2006).

Arranging the virtual space is an important aspect of preparation for a VAL set. In a synchronous session, this can include arriving in the virtual space in advance to check the technology, and welcoming set members perhaps with a welcome slide and some music. This has a practical function of allowing arriving members to test their visual and audio settings.

Table 4.1 Issues of design, facilitation and organizational learning in VAL

	Design	Facilitation	Organizational Learning
People	Language barriers and cultural written norms	Understanding the appropriateness of boundaries for online communication	Levels of online trust in the organization
	Developing a social presence	The development of virtual communication skills such as higher levels of listening and sensing skills	Permission for the participants to be 'away from the workplace' whilst at work
	Understand the working conditions or norms in the organization, e.g. hours of work/ weekend working		The understanding of the political landscape of the organization
		The ability to learn new skills	

Process	Assigning passwords	Understand the expectations regarding collaboration	Capturing the data retained by on online environment to inform organizational practice
	Time zones and equality for participants		
		Creating clear agenda and summarizing at key points	
	Managing the electronic traces of the set meetings		Intertwining off and online activity so that it's not just using the process to determine practice but also how practice creates new knowledge
	Development of online protocols	Making sure everyone is heard	
	The legislative requirements for online communication possibly more so in stranger groups	Develop reflexivity and social knowledge construction via unpacking and deconstructing the words develop the collective ability to reflect publically online	
			The development of individual or set online learning logs
Technology	Technology access and reliability	Using technical solution with the group to check emotions or 'nods'– for example posting emoticons	
	All set members have access to equal and compatible systems		

(*Continued overleaf*)

Using existing technology where possible	Tried and tested technologies, e.g. telephone conferencing may be better than sophisticated netmeeting sites that promise much but take time to master and may not deliver.
Preparation of participants regarding the technology and their own mental preparation for the meetings	
Technology preparation and training of the adviser	

Ground rules assume even more importance in a virtual setting; as well as any f2f ones, they may also include for example:

- switching off other internet facilities – email, twitter etc.;
- the way members notify the group if they are leaving the space;
- what to do if connection is lost;
- speaking more slowly and being patient for responses;
- signalling listening by using polls and emoticons;
- the use of materials created during the meeting.

After the meeting is over, tidying up the virtual environment means deciding what to do with any whiteboard work or chat files and to delete polls and any other supplementary materials.

VAL has already grown strongly and, along with virtual leadership in general, can be expected to grow further (Caulat 2012). It is likely to increase in importance in any action learning adviser's practice.

Virtual leadership

These new habits and skills of virtual working can be very effective. Working alone and in a quiet space, whilst simultaneously being in attentive communication with others, may produce more productive outcomes than the busy and distracted face-to-face meetings to which we are more used. This possibility leads to a theory of virtual leadership (Caulat 2012). If VAL works, then why should this way of working not apply to all situations where people are geographically dispersed and must organize themselves by remote communications? Virtual working has the advantages of bringing the best 'brains' to the most demanding tasks wherever they are located, whilst also greatly reducing the various costs and stresses – personal, organizational and environmental – involved in global organizing.

Because virtual leadership necessarily emphasizes relationships and not just tasks, it may develop the leadership in unexpected ways. The virtual leader must learn to put much of her effort into building and maintaining relationships, and this emphasis promotes reflexivity and search for personal authenticity. Personal integrity and continuing self-development seem essential in leadership for tackling the intractable organizational and social problems, and virtual leadership – happening in the 'moments' of facilitation between us – is one of the new ways of working to help that happen.

My practice notes 4

The set adviser or facilitator

Make some notes on this aspect of the action learning adviser's role as it relates to your current practice. You may want to consider such questions as:

- *Is this a part of what I do now? Should it be?*

- *Which aspect of the role appeals to me most?*

- *Which aspects do I find more difficult or questionable?*

- *What are my priorities for development?*

Do I create the right 'communicative spaces' for set meetings?

What about my role during the set meeting and thinking about the meeting process, including the different focus of action learning?

How are my facilitation skills including questioning, listening, challenging and supporting?

How are my skills in reflecting, reviewing, recording?

How do I deal with the problem of ending or withdrawing?

What do I want to do about VAL?

Reflection on *My practice notes 4*:

Reading through what I have just written on these aspects of the facilitator role, what does it say about me and my practice?

Deller Business Services

A case study in advising on action learning

PART 2

Part 1 – Design: what happened next

After your meeting with the Executive Team of Deller Business Services at which you proposed a design for an action learning programme (see end of Chapter 3), and a number of consequent discussions, the following design was agreed:

Directors' launch

As a consequence of being invited to be co-designers, the directors decided to spend a day together to focus on the programme and to develop a shared understanding of the desired outcomes. This involved them coming to that day with several organizational projects which they were personally prepared to sponsor. They also identified a need to spend some time thinking about what a sponsor actually does.

Programme launch

As it proved logistically impossible to get all the directors and managers together on the same date, the launch eventually took place on two separate events. The purpose of the launch events was to create a shared understanding of action learning, the proposed programme, the place of the projects and the roles of the sponsors and facilitator. The managers were invited to select sets in which to work based on the principle of a maximum mix of disciplines in each set.

Each of the directors presented projects that they would sponsor personally. As the launch was held over two days the projects were held open for bids for one week. Managers were invited to select individual projects that were sponsored by someone other than their line manager.

Managers meet sponsors

Managers were asked to arrange an appointment to meet with the sponsor of their chosen project and agree the scope prior to the first set meeting.

Action learning sets

Starting with the launch event, the ten action learning sets of about six managers were asked to meet monthly over a year. Each set had a 'budget' of three facilitated meetings, after which the facilitator would withdraw. A review summit or conference was held after the first three set meetings, and a second one three meetings later. A final event would celebrate the end of the programme.

Final event

The final summit was co-designed by the directors and managers to evaluate the outcomes in terms of action and learning, and to enjoy a dinner together to celebrate success.

The agreed design

Directors' launch

Content:

- The programme outline
- 'Past, Present & Future' shared meaning exercise
- Introduction to action learning
- Role of the sponsor
- 100 projects identified

Programme launch for managers and directors

Content:

- The programme outline
- 'Past, Present & Future' shared meaning exercise
- Introduction to action learning
- Role of the sponsor

- Role of the set adviser
- Create sets
- Projects outlined

Managers meet sponsors

Content:

- 60 managers choose projects
- Meet and agree project outline with the director who is sponsor
- Participants working with a director who is not the line manager

Set meetings

Content:

- Ten sets with nine set meetings – one each month
- Review dates set every three months
- Facilitator to withdraw after four meetings

Final event

Content:

- Co-designed by directors and participants
- To be a celebration and evaluation of achievements of both individuals and sets

Part 2 – Set advising

The programme began with the action learning sets meeting at various sites. The meetings were well attended and energetic and the plan for the facilitator to withdraw and the sets to become self-facilitated was on track. Directly before the first summit review and three months into the programme, the action learning adviser received requests for meetings from three different groups, the directors, the participating managers and the union representatives.

In these meetings, the following concerns were raised about the programme:

Managers

- not having enough time to work on the projects because of the day-to-day workload;
- finding time to meet with the sponsor;
- discovering that the sponsoring director was 'better' than their own line director;
- having torn loyalties between their 'day jobs' and project work;
- their staff feeling left out of what was happening – 'what can we tell them?' vs confidentiality of the set discussions;
- having raised expectations of career progression in the company;
- fears that their increased confidence is seen as threatening by other managers or by line manager.

Directors

- some competition between directors in terms of whose projects are succeeding;
- a better sense of each other as leaders and managers;
- their perceptions of the abilities of some managers were being challenged;
- a fear that the programme was running out of their control as the managers become more confident;
- a growing sense that as directors they could not handle all the projects;
- a recognition that this project was having an impact on the wider company.

Unions/staff

- a lack of information and clarity of what was happening;
- managers seen talking to each other outside their normal work relationships 'huddles in cafes';
- a fear that there was major change being talked about without their knowledge;
- uncertainty caused by managers doing projects/work outside their normal scope of activity;
- managers going to meetings with directors who were not their line manager (i.e. sponsor);

- staff being asked to take on extra work to cover for their manager's absence.

Task 2

Reflecting on these concerns and your reading of Chapter 4, how would you respond?

Make some notes on:

(i) What needs to happen next?

(ii) What design changes – if any – will you propose?

(You will find a response to this task at the end of the next chapter.)

5 The organization developer

Chapter overview

Developing organizational learning can be the most difficult aspect of the adviser's role, but it also carries the greatest potential for action learning. Revans' ambition was for the improvement and development of organizations for the benefit of all those who depend upon them. To achieve this he saw every organization as a prospective learning community where each member learned with and from colleagues as they tackled their problems and challenges.

The importance of this part of the action learning adviser's role is in facilitating organizational learning via the sharing of new ideas and insights from individual action learners and their sets with the wider system. These opportunities for organizational learning present themselves in two main ways: first through the activities of individual action learners, whose attempts to change inevitably involve other people in the organization or system under study, who are thus recruited to the project; and secondly when action learning sets share and exchange their findings with other organizational members, perhaps in conferences or virtually via bulletin boards.

By working with both the sets and the sponsoring managers, an adviser can promote learning conversations which can lead to useful changes without threatening normal functioning. This chapter contains advice and methods for creating such 'middle ground frameworks' and for promoting organizational learning. This chapter also contains the last part of Deller Business Services, *where once again you are invited to test your knowledge and skills in the action learning adviser's role.*

This chapter contains:

- Introduction
- Developing the learning organization
- Developing organizational learning
- Learning architectures

- Conclusion
- My practice notes 5
- Case study: Deller Business Services – Part 3

Introduction

> *Survival is not compulsory.*
>
> Attributed to W. Edwards Deming

The guru of total quality and the founder of action learning had much in common. Born in the dawn of the twentieth century and living until the end of it, or just beyond, they lived long lives and never stopped working. Both were trained in the values of science and were fond of quoting the Bible. Both believed that organizations unable to learn do not survive and that fear is the enemy of initiative taking. Both were passionately concerned with improving organizations for the benefit of society.

In his thinking about learning organizations, Revans spoke often of the need for the 'upward communication of doubt'. He saw this as an essential to aid the learning of the people at the top of any enterprise. His most concise description of the learning organization, 'Doubt ascending speeds wisdom from above' proposes that the capacity of senior managers to make the best decisions depends upon the supply of good questions flowing up from those engaged in tackling the tasks, challenges and problems of the business. This is a neat idea, but one perhaps more honoured in the breach than in the observance. As one manager wryly commented: 'In this company, doubt ascending speeds retribution from above!'

The Organisational Readiness Questionnaire in Chapter 3 is a means of testing the temperature of the water for action learning. This chapter builds upon that preparatory work to show how action learning can be a powerful means for helping organizations to improve their quality of service and to achieve their purposes. In particular it is concerned with how action learning might contribute to the idea of the learning organization and to a wider professional learning.

Developing the learning organization

Action learning provides a discipline to enable the development of good working habits. These include tackling the difficult issues, seizing the risky opportunities, questioning the status quo and experimenting with new ideas. Whether these habits will be welcomed and spread out beyond any pioneers depends greatly on the encouragement they get from people above the level of those involved. This encouragement is not guaranteed. Amazing though it may seem to the detached observer, the questioning of management policies and decisions is still seen as inappropriate in many quarters, where fear reigns and prevents the voicing of any suggestions for improvement (see Box 5.1). The owner of this pharmacy chain was a successful businessman and a strong character. He did not really expect to be questioned or to have new ideas proposed, and he couldn't see why this might be desirable. The pharmacy managers acted accordingly.

Box 5.1 The successful pharmacist

In a privately owned pharmacy group, the owner and managing director was puzzled by the largely passive nature of his monthly management meetings. He seemed to do 95 per cent of the talking whilst his assembled shop managers had little to say.

He remarked upon this to a visiting consultant, who asked: 'when were you last questioned on some aspect of company policy?' The owner was puzzled: 'I can't remember that ever happening', he finally said. 'Our pharmacy managers are not really interested in business issues, they are more concerned with ethical practice.'

Yet when the consultant conducted a series of short interviews with the shop managers, a different picture appeared. Several people had ideas in their heads; ideas that they had either read about or seen being used elsewhere; ideas that they would have liked to have tried out at work. When asked why they had not suggested these ideas at management meetings, they could not say.

This case shows some of the limits of action learning; it does not fit all situations at all times. For example, organizations which have strong training traditions, perhaps because of their technical expertise, do not necessarily or easily welcome action learning. Action learning needs significant organizational problems or opportunities to work on, together with people who are willing to set it up.

Even where bosses want to encourage people to question things, it can be surprisingly difficult. Where there is no tradition of participation, getting started on this is hard to do. Even in professional firms or public service organizations such as schools, hospitals or social work departments, openly questioning things is often seen as 'career limiting' and something attempted only by the brave or foolish. Many organizations with traditional management styles continue to survive and even to prosper, as in the pharmacy chain above, but when they find themselves in difficult conditions brought about by economic recession, changing markets or fierce and unexpected competition these traditions can become serious 'learning disabilities' (Senge 1990: 17–27). The pharmacy chain above continued prosperously for the owner for some years, however, when he wanted to retire, none of his children wanted to follow him, and none of his managers would lead a buyout, so the chain was sold to a larger one with a subsequent loss of some shops and jobs.

Action learning sets out to foster cultures of enquiry and experiment. From this perspective it is normal for able and intelligent people to reflect on what they are doing, and the questioning of working practices and processes is a sign of health and fitness. Questioning tends to produce energy: to get things done, to develop new ideas, and to seek new knowledge (see Box 5.2).

Box 5.2 Questioning catches on in a tyre factory

Action learning was brought into a tyre factory in an attempt to re-energize middle and senior management, but the workforce was cynical over the help that could be given through the self-help 'sets'. After a couple of months, however, they started to copy, unofficially, the regular and rigorous set meetings to help them solve their shop-floor problems. The senior managers quickly realized that this should be encouraged and, despite some initial union opposition, it has become the style for working and learning throughout the company.

Source: Garratt (1990: 72)

The most interesting aspect of this story is the way the shop-floor teams picked up the idea for themselves. Action learning will work wherever people want to do it; the trick is to create the conditions where this voluntary and self-initiated impulse can flower. In this example action learning catches on through a sort of osmosis and not through deliberate intent. Where this happens due to some internal capacity for learning in that setting, this is very much to be celebrated. It seems to be part of the human condition that ideas and practices that are picked up or even 'stolen' in this way, often work better than those that are given or provided.

For those situations less blessed with creative 'thieves', a more systematic programme of change and learning might be indicated.

Developing organizational learning

The term 'organizational learning' can create confusion. It offends common sense: how can an organization be said to learn, when surely only people can learn? However, as Argyris and Schön famously point out, the consequences for an organization which is unable to learn from its individual members can be very serious: 'Organizational learning is not the same thing as individual learning ... There are too many cases in which organizations know less than their members. There are even cases in which the organization cannot seem to learn what every member knows' (1978: 9).

This suddenly makes good sense. Corporate failures and scandals appear with increasing regularity, and when the reviews are published we learn that some people had their doubts about current policies or knew all along what was wrong. Sometimes these people tried to make their voices heard, but ultimately the 'organization' (or the powerful people at the top) failed to learn from them, often with dire consequences not just for those powerful few, but for many other employees, customers and neighbours.

Part of Revans' vision for action learning is to help organizations transform themselves into 'learning communities' and 'learning systems' (2011: 70, 111–20), so that (in a hospital) 'the learning virus injected into a few of the senior staff had diffused down to the bedside and into the laundry' (2011: 70).

Opportunities for organizational learning through action learning come principally from:

1   the activities of action learners as individuals, whose attempts at change influence other people along the way. For example, Revans estimates that the 21 managers on the Belgian Inter-University Programme influenced over 200 senior managers in the participating enterprises (2011: 71).

2   the exchange of experience and sharing of learning between action learning sets and other people in the organization or system, often in conferences or via bulletin boards and discussion forums. Feedback from the work of sets as collectives can sometimes be more easily heard than the lone voices of critics or whistleblowers.

In Chapter 3, we discussed the development of the organization as a learning community as the ultimate aim of the accoucheur as the designer of action learning. The important work here is in the creation of linkages between the powerful but small sets and the wider organization or system.

Whilst sets tend to be inner focused and mainly concerned with their members' goals, a good action learning programme can connect sets to these wider systems and encourage collaborative ways of working with other sets and groupings. A good programme design might use conferences to bring sets together with the key people outside the sets who have been recruited as clients and sponsors. Various communications systems and electronic networks can be employed to help with the exchange of learning and the dissemination of ideas. Where such a programme works well, the impact of action learning can have a cultural effect system-wide, and not just felt by a small number of set members.

In the case example in Box 5.3, the directors of the Health Board in Ireland set out to improve the learning capabilities of the organization and to change the way that people did things. In this action learning programme, all the managers were enrolled in self-managed sets, with the intention of influencing the operating culture of the whole enterprise.

Box 5.3 Developing organizational capability in Ireland

Brighton University's Management Development Research Unit (MDRU) was approached by a senior manager (and former student) to help organize a self-managed action learning (SMAL) programme for the 400 managers in the Health Board in Ireland. The SMAL approach was chosen because of the prohibitive cost of using facilitators from Brighton.

The first cohort of 40 managers began their year-long SMAL programme with a five day foundation workshop to help them with their self-managing of the process. This workshop covered the core values of action learning and guidelines for running and facilitating set meetings. Following this, the first two set meetings were facilitated by an external adviser. After that the sets were on their own, although, if they encountered problems, they could request a further session with an adviser. Four months after the first workshop, a *process review* was held to reflect on how the self-managed sets were working, to share learning and to develop action plans to address any identified problems. After the 12 months, a final workshop helped participants to evaluate their progress and to share their learning.

The SMAL approach raises various challenges: what are the skills of self-facilitation? And how can participants develop them? What happens if the sets run into difficulties? SMAL shifts the focus from developing skills for *facilitation* towards developing the skills for *participation*. To self-manage successfully all set members need the skills of *questioning, listening, reflection, giving and receiving feedback, creative problem solving, understanding group processes* and *understanding learning processes.* There are some other skills which are best described as management rather than facilitation skills. Typically the facilitator takes responsibility for making arrangements but in a SMAL set the members take it on themselves to contact each other to arrange meetings, fix times and places, and make all the decisions about the way the set works.

Three hundred and eighty managers participated in some 60 SMAL sets over a period of four years. The external evaluation report concluded that the programme was: 'a very humanising experience. Our overall view was that the programme was positive and courageous in changing the culture of the Health Board. The results are exceptional.' 'The management development programme has had considerable beneficial influence on the individuals who have attended and on their colleagues in the organisation' (Tamkin 2000).

The Health Board itself carried out a major research project to evaluate the outcomes and concluded that: 'All the research carried out to date identifies behaviour and attitude change and an ability to deal with situations differently.' This study stated that the work undertaken by the SMAL participants in the form of change projects 'had developed the organisation's capacity to meet the challenge of implementing the Quality and Fairness Initiative' (a major change initiative for Irish Health Boards) (Murphy 2003).

Source: Adapted with permission from Bourner (2011)

The Irish Health Board example is impressive not only for its ambition but also for the large scale trial of the self-managed model of action learning. Any extensive programme of action learning is likely to run up against the questions of costs, especially the costs of experienced set advisers or facilitators. But there are other reasons to think about the decision to make set self-managing, including the fact that this is Revans' own preference. Another compelling reason is that it frees the time and resources of the action learning adviser to concentrate on those aspects of the role that cannot be delegated, namely the design of action learning interventions and the harvesting and dissemination of the learning from these activities.

Learning architectures

To sustain an action learning effort over the time needed to bring about cultural changes requires ideas for structuring relationships and dialogues beyond the small group level. This means thinking about what is needed apart from action learning sets. This is quite a task for the adviser, not only because it is practically difficult work, but because of the centrality of the idea of the set in action learning. It is hard to overstate the importance of this idea. The set is, at one and the same time, the guiding vision and the practical method that creates 'the cutting edge of every action learning programme' (Revans 2011: 7). Yet the set alone cannot bring about Revans' vision of the organization or the whole system as a learning community. To tackle this ambition the action learning adviser will need to invent more tools and social technologies such as the conferencing discussed in Chapter 3.

These social tools and technologies can be grouped under the concept of a 'learning architecture'. This idea can be simply expressed as: 'the way an organization promotes and structures learning, both individual and organizational' (Wilhelm 2005: 9). But this implies that the leadership of any organization has given conscious and collective thought to the idea. Perhaps not too many senior teams sit around and ask themselves the question: 'Now what should be our learning architecture?' According to Wilhelm (2005: 14) the person who does do this is the CLO or 'chief learning officer'. As this might be a good way to make sure no one else takes it seriously, we are nominating the action learning adviser, who has hopefully laid the groundwork for this systemic learning in the accoucheur phase.

Action learning can be a key component in a wider learning architecture which has the ultimate aim of helping the organization achieve its purposes through becoming a learning organization. Whilst the 'what' of change and learning can't be pre-specified, the process of change management and learning can be mapped out in advance. Figure 5.1 depicts a learning architecture in a large concern where the action learning sets are embedded in a wider process including conferences and other events.

In this example, action learning is embedded in a regular sequence and cycle of other activities for planning and learning. An annual stakeholder event looks at the overall strategy and sets the context for a planning conference which reviews the company's goals and direction. From these events, a design team facilitates the formation of action learning sets to tackle problems and opportunities which will hopefully move the organization forward on various fronts. The activities of the action learning sets generate learning and ideas for future events, and feed into the annual cycle of review, experiment and renewal.

Obviously this sort of learning architecture is only possible with the considerable backing and collaboration of senior people. The leadership team in particular have an important part to play in various stages of the process outlined in Figure 5.1. The discussion below touches on some of

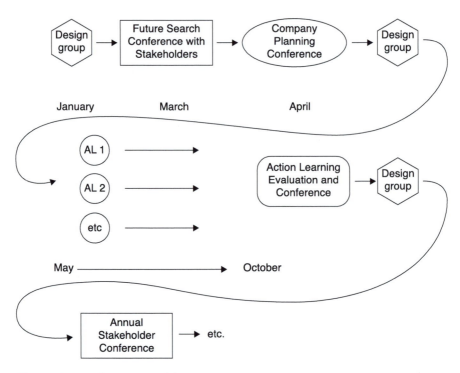

Figure 5.1 A learning architecture

the main components of a learning architecture (Attwood et al. 2003), namely:

- design teams
- leadership teams
- dialogue and 'public learning'
- middle-ground frameworks
- widening circles of learning

Design teams

Action learning programmes of any size and duration need to be crafted over time to respond to emerging issues. The initial task of designing the activities and their sequencing, and also the ongoing facilitation and re-design of the initiative, are tasks which can be usefully shared with a design or support team.

Design teams should include delegates from the key groups concerned, including participants and sponsors, and should aim to represent the whole system in which the programme is operating. The design team also handles or oversees the logistics, communication and evaluation processes, and can work as an action learning set itself, testing proposals in action and learning from them to achieve the best programme possible. A design team has to balance 'the trains running on time' with being alert to re-design opportunities generated by the action and learning processes.

In the case example in Box 5.4 there are two levels of design team; a national level formed from area-based facilitators (ABFs) and a regional one formed from local facilitators in each region.

Box 5.4 Organizing action learning in the NHS pathology services

This Department of Health sponsored project to promote learning and change in UK pathology services through action learning ran from September 2006 to January 2008. It operated in six regions of England through area-based facilitators (ABFs) whose task was to initiate and support regional sets, including the recruitment and training of local set facilitators. Some ABFs were much more successful than others, partly due to the nature of their 'patch' and partly due to their own skills, resources and networks.

Discussions in the regular ABFs' meeting showed wide variations in their initiation practices. Most ABFs were working in their own regions with existing networks that proved very useful especially where they were linked to others in the worlds of service improvement and learning and development. Other significant differences between ABFs emerged in their beliefs about the initiation process, and in how persistent they were in making links and enthusing people in pathology services.

Some sets were established quickly and opportunistically; others took six or even nine months to negotiate via building relationships and holding introductory meetings in complex conditions. Generally speaking, it was these latter sets that lasted longer and were more successful than those with shallower roots. At this time the ABFs were acting as accoucheurs, focused on getting sets established, rather than taking on the more familiar role of set facilitators. Some who were more used to and skilled in the set facilitation role, found this uncomfortable at first and took time to adapt. Good conversations about ways of handling this happened in the regular ABF meetings, for example around such issues as managing the paradox of being neither too close nor too distant from the local facilitators: supporting and coaching them where necessary but not getting between them and their sets.

Regional action learning architectures

The ABFs were encouraged to establish connections between the sets within their regions. Again this proved easier in some places than in others, and always took different forms. In the West Midlands, an oversight group chaired by a senior manager from the Strategic Health Authority, encouraged and steered the work of the sets, connected them into mainstream agendas and prompted a regional conference of set members and other interested people. In the North East, the sets were sponsored by a well established pathology network which helped to organize the sets around key themes in its development agenda.

Local facilitators' sets were an important part of the regional architecture and, facilitated by the ABFs, existed in varying degrees of formality. As well as their main purpose in supporting the local sets of pathology clinicians and managers, they also were a developmental forum for the local facilitators. It was generally agreed that these regional forums were critical to keeping the initiative going sustainability and to generally increasing the capacity of the local pathology system to deal with complex service change.

Source: Department of Health/Pathology Modernisation (2008)

When there is a design team or teams that are working well, it means that the success of the programme no longer rests solely on the skills and capacities of the action learning adviser. Such a team not only brings added skills and resources, but generally has much better intelligence about the system in which they are working, than any adviser operating alone.

Leadership teams

Leadership teams play an important part in any learning architecture, especially in 'fronting up' the various public gatherings or conferences, in presenting the current situation, strategy and direction and in receiving feedback and views from the assembly. The surprises and unforeseen issues likely to emerge through action learning, mean that the leadership team needs to be seen to respond to any significant questions or challenges that arise.

In a business, the directors, or a subset of them, might make up the leadership team. In a public service organization or network, partnership or community setting, the leadership team may be formed by representatives from the important stakeholders to the venture. Whatever the composition, this team is likely to need coaching and support to help them respond well to emerging questions and challenges. There is often a fine balance to be struck between pointing out the constraints and defining the givens in any situation, and encouraging people to take initiatives, seize opportunities and generally to test out their ideas in action.

To assemble, brief and facilitate a design team is a relatively simple task in any situation, but finding a leadership team willing, able and generally 'up' for this role may be more problematic. The leadership role involves more exposure than is normal for many senior managers. It puts them on the line in terms of being the guardians of the existing strategy and at the same time opening the door to new ideas and initiatives for change. The leadership team needs courage and confidence but also the humility to encourage open exchanges and seek feedback on their actions and policies.

This sort of learning in public is very demanding for anyone, and especially perhaps for leaders. But if it can be achieved, it will convince everyone present more than anything else. Nothing is more powerful than leaders visibly learning.

Dialogue and 'public learning'

In 'public learning' (Attwood et al. 2003: 32–3, 77–94), insights and breakthroughs happen in public. Where questions and challenges are voiced, and where leaders make it plain that they do not have all the answers, when they think aloud and show themselves as struggling to come to grips with the new, then the space is created for everyone to learn. The sight of leaders as learners seeking new insights and meanings along with others is a compelling example.

A learning architecture can create opportunities for action learners to be in dialogue with the leadership team, perhaps from the collective safety of the set. The action learning adviser then has the chance to facilitate this dialogue, as in the model we saw in Chapter 2 (see Figure 5.2).

An example of this sort of dialogue can be found in Chapter 6, in 'The Gladwell story' (pp. 127–30) where exchanges between the leadership and the action learners resulted in much learning despite being very frank and even heated. Open and public dialogue demands equality of voice and the right to be heard, and if this is to happen in the context of

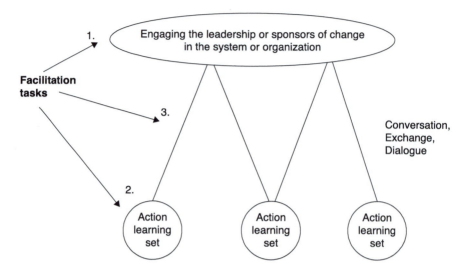

Figure 5.2 Facilitating dialogue between action learning sets and the leadership team

an organizational structure, then the normal operating procedures of rank and hierarchy must be temporarily suspended. For this to happen it may be necessary to invent a 'middle-ground framework'.

Middle-ground frameworks

This idea is a response to the problem in organizational learning of bringing together the knowledge of the people leading the enterprise with the local knowledge and know-how of those making the product or delivering the service (Attwood et al. 2003: 50–1). A good exchange of views enables all parties to get a better view of the situation by accessing information and opinions not normally available to them, and in turn enables more informed action in their respective domains.

The word 'framework' has perhaps too solid a ring; in the Gladwell Case (Chapter 6) this consists of a series of conversations between the executive team and the action learners. Crucially, these meetings start with an invitation from the action learners, and equally crucially they take place not in the Chief Executive's office but on the action learners' turf. Middle-ground frameworks may be constructed spontaneously in this way, or can be programmed in to provide regular opportunities for exchange. However, if they are programmed meetings, then care

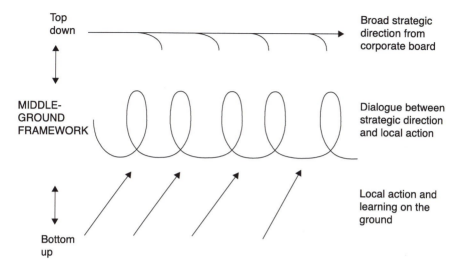

Figure 5.3 A middle-ground framework

must be taken to maintain the essentially temporary nature of such 'scaffoldings'. Middle-ground frameworks tend to work for a time, perhaps only once or twice in any one form, and if institutionalized, may quickly lose their potential for open exchange. Figure 5.3 is a simple illustration of this idea.

Widening circles of learning

Any framework that achieves engagement and exchange across different parts of an organization or system helps to spread learning. Another key organizational learning problem is the Curate's Egg or 'patches of excellence' phenomenon, where some parts of the system learn and innovate, but others do not. Because departments and units may work in relative isolation they may not know of such differences, which only become obvious when they are linked in a supply chain or patient's journey. When this chain linkage is important, then even one ineffective part has a negative impact on the whole.

In an integrated service or system there is little value in learning in patches unless this can be shared and spread. As the developer of wider organizational learning, the action learning adviser is always on the lookout for the prospects for widening circles of learning (Figure 5.4).

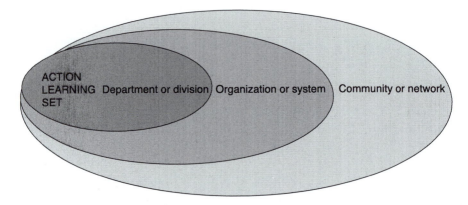

Figure 5.4 Widening circles of learning

As with the middle-ground framework, which is a specific means for sharing learning across organizational levels, there are many different ways of encouraging action learning sets to widen their circles of learning. These can include conferences, knowledge cafes, expos where groups offers their ideas at stalls, websites and other electronic networks. Any aspiring learning organization is concerned to encourage this sharing and spreading, and the action learning adviser can contribute to this by designing the action learning so that it contributes to such wider purposes.

Conclusion

This chapter has focused on the action learning adviser's role as the facilitator of organizational learning and especially upon the sharing and spreading of learning from the work of individual learners and their sets to the wider organization, community or system. However, whilst some enterprises aspire to be learning organizations which facilitate the learning of all their members and are able to change themselves as whole when that is necessary and appropriate, many fall short of this ideal. Any action learning adviser working at this level will realize that useful learning often extends beyond and across organizational boundaries and that this learning is a valuable asset both to individuals and their employers.

At the present time, with rapid technological developments and shifting balances of power between nations, it makes little sense to limit learning to what goes on inside organizations. 'Knowledge workers' whose currency rests on being up to date and resourceful, must more and more operate across and beyond business and even national boundaries to stay with the game. And the webs of connection between such people do not only serve specific professionals purposes, but are increasingly a new way of organizing. Network organizing is a natural partner for action learning; a theme which is developed in Chapter 7.

 My practice notes 5

Developing wider organizational learning

Make some notes on this third aspect of the action learning adviser's role as it relates to your current practice. You may want to consider such questions as:

- *Is this a part of what I do now? Should it be?*

- *Which aspect of the organizational develop role appeals to me most?*

- *Which aspects do I find less useful or impractical?*

- *What are my priorities for my own development in this aspect of the action learning adviser's role?*

What about my role in . . .

- developing the learning organization and organizational learning?

- designing and facilitating learning architectures?

- encouraging communities and network learning?

Reflection on *My practice notes 5* above:
Reading through what I have just written on these aspects of the organizational developer role, what does it say about me and my practice?

Deller Business Services

A case study in advising on action learning

PART 3

Part 2 – Set advising: what happened next

The timing of the first review summit proved highly fortuitous in allowing these concerns and issues to be discussed. Union representatives were invite to the summit to hear presentations and talk to the action learning sets.

As a result of the discussions, the following design changes were agreed:

1 The directors would start their own action learning set facilitated by the adviser.
2 A 'Business Improvements' blog will be set up on the Deller intranet to allow all staff to view and comment on the programme and the progress of projects.
3 A 'Talking Wall' will be installed in the staff canteen where comments can be posted and projects updated weekly with news from each set.
4 Future reviews will be joint summits with directors and participating managers.
5 All action learning sets are asked to think about their relationships and impact on those outside the set.
6 All action learning sets are asked to consider the organizational development opportunities of the programme and how these can fed back to the directors at the review summits.

Part 3 – Organizational and professional learning

An informal evaluation study completed some three years later, asked the participants and the directors, together with some representatives from staff and customers, for their comments on the outcomes of the action learning programme.

The main findings and comments that resulted from this email survey are as follows:

1 Substantive outcomes

- The large majority of the projects that were started were considered by the directors to have been completed successfully.
- Of the ten action learning sets established, all lasted the programme and eight continued, sometimes for up to six months after it finished.
- Ten managers who have since been promoted cited the programme as a key reason for their success.
- Five managers and one director have since voluntarily left the organization and one manager has been dismissed. The programme was cited as a significant factor in these decisions.

2 Directors' feedback

'I had one member of staff that to be honest I felt was treading water to retirement and half hoping that might be forced. It was a joke in the Executive team that if the business improvement project could energize him then it would be a piece of magic – a real challenge to the facilitator. Well it did – I had feedback from his sponsor and I couldn't believe it was the same person. When I spoke to him he said I had never given him a chance to show what he could do – I had written him off as stuck in his ways. I spent two months after the programme finished trying to persuade him to stay on but he didn't. I still feel guilty about the way I treated him.'

'The projects were all challenging – and the managers embraced them – I was concerned that my managers were spending too much time on them and not focusing on their day job. I don't think we were prepared for the energy the programme unleashed. I think we tried to rein it back but it was too late – we had lost control. The OD director left – he got an international posting and I guess I still feel betrayed by that – was this a promotion interview programme for him.'

'The programme started really well – the objective was clear to develop a more commercial culture. The programme released an energy that we at director level were just unaware of. That became a contested point at executive team meetings to the point the programme was almost stopped. As a group we were simply not working together. One director became very popular with the managers – he is very dynamic and the rest of us started to see this as a competition for "best project outcome" or most "popular director". By the time we had our own set these positions had become entrenched and I believe there was a lot of cold conflict that even with the support of the facilitator we couldn't seem to address. After a while I think we went into self destruct mode and the team did break up – the self-facilitated sets just couldn't work with the levels of mistrust.'

'The programme was expensive to run and the stakes were high. Would we have reached the same outcome by just setting up project teams? I think so. Would we have seen the skills abilities and weaknesses of our managers? I don't think so. Was it a development opportunity for managers? Yes, although I am a firm believer that an MBA programme would have done all that and we would have had an external validation for decisions about future prospects of staff.'

'We made a big mistake in "letting go" of the facilitator. It was planned that she would go once the programme was up and running. What we didn't see or recognize was the energy she put in to maintain the momentum and how much the relationship that was building between the exec team and managers was down to her work. We thought we could do it alone – and of course there was financial pressure to do so.'

3 Managers' feedback

'I would have liked a choice as to whether to participate – interesting that we had to do this but the executive team didn't – so they are so wonderful – in that case why after one year were we making people redundant because ill thought through projects had cost the organization so much money? I am not saying I didn't enjoy the experience – I did I met new people and we got on really well and we still keep in touch even though some have left.'

I really liked having a female facilitator – she was inspirational. We had no female role models as directors and yet the organization is primarily female. She was open and shared her history with us and I realized that I could control my career and I was the only one who could. I became more challenging and did take risks – I am now a director two years on and hope I can be the inspiration to other women.'

'My project went really well and saved the organization a lot of money – I got on really well with my project sponsor and he tried to poach me for his team – it was very flattering.'

'While we had a facilitator everything went really well – the projects were on target – relationships with the sponsors were strong and I felt as though I was really developing an understanding of this new culture. Then we were left to self facilitate – it just didn't work. We had lots of fun but we didn't get anywhere. As a group we missed the link between the set and the directors. To be honest we thought she (the facilitator) had an easy job in the set. What we missed was the way she was able to make the link between us and the executive team. So in our set only three of the six succeeded – what a waste.'

'My sponsor wasn't really committed – he thought I should be doing an MBA – the fact I had one escaped his notice. I was very angry and frustrated – others seemed to getting on really well and me I had the commitment but needed the sponsor. When I challenged him he said nobody could sort out the mess that represented my project it was a waste of time. With commitment like that who is going to carry on? I didn't.'

'My sponsor just didn't have the time for this programme. He had eight projects he was sponsoring and although he made all the right noises he just wasn't around as soon as the facilitator left the programme. I remember the CEO saying to me in the corridor how lucky I was to have a XXXXX as a sponsor – I didn't know what to say.'

'I loved the whole experience – I developed as a manager and completed the project, a double triumph. I did not have a lot of confidence and people in my section (housekeeping) were thought of as not being very bright and that included me! I took a project to develop the commercial use of one of the historical buildings the company owned. My fellow set members were very surprised that I was classed as a manager at first and was joining the group. But over the meetings as I listened to others issues I realized I did have a lot to offer. I had to develop a case for investment to refurbish the building for use as a conference and wedding venue. I think my sponsor was a bit dismayed when I was chosen to do this project – he said afterwards he wanted someone from finance – but he agreed afterward that the finance side was pretty much mechanistic. Anyway it put me and my team in the spotlight when it (the project) was highlighted in the company newsletter. It did us all good, and me well, I am a regional facilities manager now.'

'My project was discontinued – I think it was too much of a challenge for the exec team. The nature of the project meant that I was consistently challenging the status quo and they were uncomfortable about that. I didn't think they expected what they got even though they said that's what they wanted. I didn't want to tinker around the edge of a bad process – I knew it needed a radical overhaul and I wasn't prepared to do anything less.'

'Our set uncovered the bad practice of one of the managers – in fact it turned out to be fraud and he was disciplined and has now left. It was a real challenge for the set in terms of confidentiality. The whole thing became very uncomfortable – particularly since throughout the disciplinary process he continued as a set member. I do think he should have been asked to leave the set whilst the investigation went on. Should we have raised that?'

4. Staff feedback

'What we started to do felt more purposeful – I think it was because the "talking wall" meant that we had a sense of what the organization was doing collectively.'

'My manager became more human – does that make sense? It was as though he started to care about what we thought.'

'Our manager was in the spot light from the Directors and she became quite superficial always wanting to be seen in the best light rather than really caring about the job. From being respected in our team she has become despised, we don't trust her anymore.'

'I started to understand what the new company was about – I didn't like it and eventually left. My manager got promotion on the basis of his project and I got his job so I think it was great!! It (the programme) did change things – the back hand dealings between managers stopped and the organization feels more honest – of course some left because their power base had gone but good riddance.'

'Was it worth the money? I don't know – we were told about the savings and increase in income but nobody talked about the cost.'

'Some managers seem to have thrived and gone on to be promoted on the basis of the projects they did – but was this just luck in the choice of project. Our manager took a really difficult project on and it didn't work – was he set up to fail – it feels like it.'

'I don't know about the learning – all we heard about was the action – the successful projects were rammed down our throats. Managers who did those became stars for a while. Those who didn't complete projects or they didn't work seemed to disappear.'

5 Customer feedback

'When we were first told about this programme to be honest we thought it was another one of those fads. I couldn't believe the person leading the project on community development was an architect – what on earth did he know about community involvement? However, it was that innocence but willingness to learn from all the members that made it so successful. When he suggested a world cafe event to seek all the members' views I thought he was mad. But it worked and we then went on to form action learning sets to look at the issues that had been brought up. He acknowledged this wasn't his skill level but was learning from his set facilitator. It was great – refreshing and what we achieved has been sustainable. Funny he retired not long after the programme finished and he is now vice chairman as a volunteer.'

'I hold our business account manager in high esteem and was surprised that someone else had been "brought in" with ittle experience of our organization to look at a project to develop a sustainable relationship over the next five years. However, she uncovered what had been custom and practice for both us and the business account manager that no longer made sense. Fortunately both got on well and we were able to redevelop the contract with ease and humour. However, I am not sure whether this was a lucky accident or planned in some way. It could have been a disaster for all of us.'

Task 3

From your reading of the comments above from participants, directors, staff and customers together with your reading of Chapter 5, reflect on the impact on the organization and people of the action learning programme.

Make some notes on:

(i) What will I do differently next time I talk to a potential new client for action learning?

(ii) Are there any points from this case that suggest I need to learn new skills or focus more on particular aspects of the action learning adviser's role?

6   Becoming critical

Chapter overview

Critical action learning (CAL) appeared in the 1990s via academics seeking a more critical approach to management education in general. Current provision, anchored around the MBA, is seen as being too rational and functionalist and action learning offers a new approach emphasizing learning from peers and from real life problems and opportunities. However, Revans' action learning is seen in danger of being 'captured by the dominant and the powerful in order to maintain the status quo. To prevent this, a more critical approach is needed, drawing on critical social theory, to help learners stand outside their organizational and cultural surroundings to ask more fundamental questions.

Critical action learning goes beyond 'ordinary criticality' to question existing practices, structures and power relations within the organization. It does this by encouraging the practices of critical thinking and reflection, and distinguishes between effective practice, reflective practice and critically reflective practice.

This chapter includes case illustrations of CAL principles being put into practice in sets and in organizations. It also offers some activities for practising the CAL approach in sets, and considers the pros and cons of encouraging critical reflection in managers. It concludes that action learners can aspire to be 'tempered radicals' – people who retain the desire to change things whilst staying committed to their organizations; people who want to rock the boat, but also want to stay in it.

This chapter contains:

- Introduction
- The case for CAL
- CAL = AL + CST?
- What does CAL look like?
- In search of organizing insight . . .
- . . . and critical spaces
- Encouraging critical reflection

- CRP: critically reflective practice
- Critical thinking: the dark side
- Action learners as tempered radicals
- Conclusion
- My practice notes 6

Introduction

Revans crafted his idea of action learning over a long life and career, with many of the key ideas coming together in the 1970s. This decade saw the emergence of his most significant books and papers, culminating in his 'collected works' – *The Origins and Growth of Action Learning* – which appeared in 1982. Critical action learning (CAL) is post-Revans, and starts to appear some ten years later from academics seeking a sharper edge for management teaching in general. The CAL writers are dissatisfied with current management education provision which they see as being too rational, functionalist and 'technicist', always concerned with the 'how' and never with the 'why'. For these writers, action learning offers a radical new approach to reclaim management education from these functionalist preoccupations. However, 'ordinary' action learning is too easily harnessed to the needs of the organization and is not critical enough for the CAL theorists. Given that action learning is easily adapted to serve local agendas, how can it avoid the trap of being 'selectively adopted to maintain the status quo' by powerful interests (Willmott 1994: 127)?

CAL sets out to understand how attempts at action and learning in human systems – organizations, communities, networks and societies – are governed and constrained by power and politics. Its practice involves engaging with these political, emotional and cultural processes to enlarge freedoms and reduce oppressions. This is dangerous and uncomfortable territory, where meanings are slippery and there is often little 'common sense', but the prize is a glittering one. This is nothing less than the promise of emancipation from old ways of seeing, thinking, doing and organizing. CAL aspires to reveal the perspectives and patterns which have become oppressive, and to generate new ways of working that liberate energies, ideas and learning. Can CAL possibly deliver? A paper (Rigg and Trehan 2008) on critical reflection in the workplace asks: is it just too difficult?

The argument for CAL has developed since the 1990s, and yet it remains a work in progress. This chapter will consider how this approach can produce learning and development that is not available through a less critical lens. As part of this, it will address the questions: 'What is CAL?' and, with more difficulty, 'How do you practise it?'

The case for CAL

How is CAL different from 'ordinary' action learning? Revans taught that action learning is not for puzzles however technically complex, but for situations where managers are in confusion, beset by anxieties and at risk. He knew that learning was a profoundly emotional process and understood that organizational politics impacts on action learning, as is evident on the attention he pays to the importance of sponsors, allies and 'structures of welcome' in organizations (1971: 85–99; 2011: 37–8, 71–4). He also observes that what is ultimately learned in action learning is the 'micropolitics' of organization (1982: 629–30; 2011: 76). However, the apparent simplicity of the action learning idea, when translated in practice, can appear naive.

Take, for example, the set which lies at the heart of action learning, and which puts its faith in the 'wisdom of peers':

> Action Learning is to make useful progress on the treatment of problems/opportunities, where no solution can possibly exist already because different managers, all honest, experienced and wise, will advocate different courses of actions in accordance with their different value systems, their different past experiences and their different hopes for the future.
>
> (Revans 2011: 24)

But do we have sufficient variety of knowledge, value systems and creative thinking? Are we consistently honest, experienced and wise? And do we advocate different actions in accordance with our different value systems whatever our organizational responsibilities, loyalties and interests?

Willmott (1994; 1997) proposes a critical action learning as a means of correcting what he sees as an unquestioning tradition in management education, where business schools promote formulaic problem solving and propose a technical 'management by numbers' approach. He wants to change this and sees action learning as having the radical potential to do this, especially because of the peer relationship and the power it puts into the hands of learners.

However, he argues that conventional action learning will not do this because managers share a dominant ideology and set of values which means that they are unlikely to question their practices from an independent standpoint. Managers are socialized into these practices and values via what Raelin (2008: 523) describes as 'cultural doping'. Given the power of corporate cultures and the pressures to conform, what chance is there of managers, especially when drawn from the same or similar concerns, being able to exert a critical view of their organizational and social worlds?

Thus, in this view, conventional action learning is all too easily 'captured' by the interests of the powerful. So, whilst this might produce some incremental improvements to organizational processes via action learning, no fundamental change is possible and any alterations will always be at the behest of those in control. It is also, in this way, possible to imagine action learning being employed to do harm. For example, it might be used to further undesirable organizational purposes such as mis-selling financial services, evading environmental restrictions on minerals extraction or promoting forms of performance management that cause stress and ill health, without these practices being questioned by participants. In these circumstances as Vince has repeatedly pointed out (2002; 2004; 2008) action learning may not lead to the 'empowerment' of the individual learner but actually the opposite.

In such conditions, we know that many managers have private doubts but that they will hesitate to voice them even in the public of the set. Watson (1994) gives many examples of these in his study of managers in a large company, but here is a recent example:

> Over dinner on a corporate programme, a rolling conversation had touched on the growing inequalities in Western society, especially in the UK and on how the 'baby boomers' (born just after the 1939–45 World War) would always be richer than their children – at least until they died! One manager reflected that he was 'a participant' in bringing this about, as it was part of his job at the moment to remove the final salary pension scheme from new starters. This caused a short pause in the conversation, which then passed on to other matters.

Does it help to bring such matters to the surface, for example in a critical action learning set? Can public reflection in democratic arenas such as the set bring about improvements in wider social structures? In a discussion of one of Watson's scenarios, Alvesson and Willmott (1996: 15–17) propose that some critical reflection might lead to a change in organizational governance systems. These are the big hopes and the big questions which must be worked out in practice.

CAL = AL + CST?

Revans would be concerned that any dollops of theory, critical or otherwise, would get in the way of the essential action which provides the basis for learning. He deliberately downplayed the role of theory in action learning; however, actions should be 'sober and deliberate', that is, thought about, weighed and deliberated. This means taking a critical stance (Box 6.1).

Box 6.1 The case for CAL (1) Developing our Critical Faculties

Practising critical thinking can . . .
. . . strengthen independence of mind
. . . add to managerial skill by developing judgement about what is important
. . . make us more aware of what counts as knowledge, and therefore of what we already know
. . . increase self-knowledge – about what assumptions we are making, how we make them and how they can be changed.

Source: Adapted from Anderson and Thorpe (2004)

CAL requires something more than ordinary criticality. In his recipe for CAL, Willmott (1997: 753) adds a supplement of critical social theory or CST:

> 'Received wisdom, including that of experts, is subject to critical scrutiny, through a fusion of reflection and insights drawn from critical social theory . . . CST is required, not just as a knowledge of some specific sets of ideas, but as a general source of political awareness and an understanding of the world as a 'psycho-political field of action and change'.

CST is a family term for idea systems such as Marxism, feminism, post-structuralism and deep ecology that challenge current social norms. Critical social theory derives its analytic power by standing against the value positions and judgements of current best practice, and thereby reveals the political and cultural dimensions of any situation.

CAL (AL + CST) draws our attention to the political purposes behind the uses of action learning. As Vince (2011) notes, there is an unresolved tension between the avowed radicalism of action learning and the political motives behind its use. Vince incorporates a psychodynamic perspective where the 'problems' of the individual mirror organizational power relationships or where any change efforts 'can be undermined . . . by a perceived need to maintain the status quo'. So for example, people may imagine that they are being offered 'development' through action learning but in fact their actions turn out to reinforce existing organizational norms and expectations. The hope is that CAL sets will help individuals to understand their complex political environments and in choosing actions, recognize how these will be affected by the power dynamics (Box 6.2).

Box 6.2 The case for CAL (2) Unmasking Administrative Evil

Evil is inherent in the human condition.

Administrative evil (from Eichmann on) is where people, in role, along with others, act and participate in what 'a critical and reasonable observer, usually well after the fact, would call evil'.

In a Modern Age, characterised by technical rationality, Administrative Evil is usually masked in many different ways, so that we may engage in acts of evil without being aware that we are doing anything wrong.

In cases of 'moral inversion', evil is defined as 'good' and ordinary people can believe that what they are doing is not only correct, but is in fact, for the good.

Source: Adams and Balfour (1998)

With these aspirations, CAL is an important development in action learning, and perhaps in management and leadership education. It promotes a deepening of critical thinking by emphasizing the value of collective as well as individual reflection on organizational life. It may help individuals, like the manager quoted above, to add to their own experiences of action (learning from experience) via a collective reflection in the set on the organizational dynamics created in action (learning from organizing). The latter process, which Vince terms 'organizing insight', is an explicit recognition of the role that politics can play in facilitating, and constraining, the scope for learning (Vince 2002).

Whilst not losing sight of Revans' doubts about the value of theory in action learning, there are powerful arguments for supporting a more critical approach. These include:

- Action learning does not always work as intended, because rather than the intended 'learning in action', people may choose 'inaction' and avoidance of learning (Vince 2008).

- Exploring the reasons for the avoidance of learning, may enable people to become more critical and independent minded, and therefore better at dealing with the intractable and 'wicked' problems of organizations and society.
- Critical awareness may help us to avoid 'administrative evil', where we do harm to others whilst 'just doing our jobs' and believing that we are in the right.

Marx's dictum: 'Our purpose is not to understand the world but to change it' applies here. The grandfather of critical theorists would have been a keen advocate of CAL. As a more recent 'critter' puts it, critical thinking is not a passive, internal process but an active enquiry: 'Critical thinking is a praxis of alternating analysis and action' (Brookfield 1987: 23). This is where the risk comes in; taking action from a critical perspective will perhaps take even more wisdom and courage, and all the help you can get from the set and any other friends in the system.

What does CAL look like?

How does CAL make a difference? It can most easily be seen at work in sets, and in the opportunities it offers to individuals for critical reflection. If the ground rules of the set allow for this, members may be encouraged to explore the tensions, contradictions, emotions and power dynamics that exist in their lives. In Box 6.3 a manager speaks about how reflective work in the set has changed their views about leadership.

Box 6.3 *Me and my leadership*

This manager was looking back on their work in the set:

By being encouraged to look at issues about my power base and my influence over others within the context of the culture of my organization and my profession, I was moving towards a critically reflective position which began to question some of my underlying assumptions about leadership as a discipline, as well as about me as an individual. However, whilst considering issues in relation to both the personal power and position power I am able to wield, I began to reflect on how inequalities and power differences within society can be mirrored in organizations, obvious examples being in relation to equality of opportunity for staff; and the need for manager/leaders to address their personal role in perpetuating these inequalities.

I hope it will make me a better leader, but in a strange way that seems less important now. The main thing is that I have given myself permission to be a real live fallible person and I like myself much better for it.
Source: Trehan and Pedler (2009: 46)

This approach to leadership development helps participants to be aware of their own theories-in-use, becoming as Carr and Kemmis put it, emancipated 'from the often unseen constraints of assumption, habit, precedent, coercion and ideology' (in Trehan and Pedler 2009: 46). It also encourages people to value their own experiences, trust their own insights and develop the confidence to develop their own theories about how their worlds work. One of the outputs of CAL then, is in helping people to create theory from their practice, and to improve their practice on the basis of their new thinking.

In addition to critical reflection, CAL reinforces the action learning values of practice and practical knowledge gained from experience, together with the importance of collaboration and collective working. Whilst these practices can also most obviously be seen in the workings of the set, if CAL is to deliver on its promises it must be seen to impact on wider social structures. The Gladwell case in Box 6.4, tells the story of an ambitious programme of community development being attempted by the Town Council and its partners.

Box 6.4 The Gladwell story

Action learning was employed as part of an attempt to introduce resident self-governance at neighbourhood level in Gladwell, a town of some 350,000 people on the edge of a major UK conurbation. In partnership with other local agencies, including the NHS, the police and voluntary organizations, the Council gained European funding over several years to contribute to the social and economic regeneration of its many deprived communities. This funding was intended to pump prime the re-direction of mainstream spending by all the agencies concerned to ensure that service delivery better reflected local priorities.

A partnership board led the initiative and employed consultants who, as part of their work, facilitated an action learning group of

seconded people were to act as 'neighbourhood facilitators' charged with helping the residents towards self governance via local neighbourhood committees. This action learning group met for a total of 15 days over a 13 month period.

Giving the Council back to the people

The neighbourhood facilitators were responsible for a community development effort which began with public meetings in seven pilot neighbourhoods. From these meetings, teams of local people were chosen to represent 'the whole system' of diverse groups and interests in each neighbourhood. These 'design teams' then had several meetings to plan two-day 'big events' which were held in each neighbourhood to build a vision for the future. After the big events, interim community forums were set up pending local elections for the neighbourhood committees.

The neighbourhood facilitators' action learning group

As the facilitators' group began work on this demanding schedule of tasks, it became clear that the ideas, purposes and background to this work were not at all clear to most people, and much early effort went into trying to make sense of what was going on. The group were attempting unfamiliar tasks with demanding deadlines, amid a great complexity of local systems and politically unstable conditions; a combination which led to many anxieties and feelings of personal insecurity.

Most people were on short-term secondments and worried about their 'day jobs'. Life in the group was difficult, exciting, depressing and joyful in turns; with various histories, personal and institutional, glimpsed from time to time but usually bobbing about under the surface.

Group development

Meetings were pressurized, overloaded with information and several emerging conflicts. From the outset the imperative for urgent action created a steep learning curve for all concerned. People had many urgent questions:

- 'I'm interested in community work but I've never been out of the Council, will I cope?'
- 'What will happen when we stand up in front of local people who are angry with us?'
- 'My manager didn't want to release me and told me I had to carry the extra workload.'

- 'How do we get them involved?' 'Who should be in a "design team"?'
- 'How committed is the Council to all this?'
- 'What's happening with the partnership board?'
- 'What logistical support do we get?'

The pace was such that these urgent preoccupations came and went very quickly. By the second meeting, a feverish concern with 'start-ups' had changed to an urgent focus on the next stages in the process – 'design teams' and 'big events' – all of which felt like ultimate goals at different times. By the third meeting the group had spent four days together in a little over three weeks and by the fourth two members had already dropped out citing 'day job' demands. But by now the group felt less fractured, more cohesive and committed. Outwardly, attention had again shifted from the stages in the process to different questions – 'Can we deliver?' and 'How much is in the pot anyway?' – and a concern not to over-promise to residents.

At this time the group reflected on the rapid progression of the group from one urgent concern to the next, and to the personal development already evident as individuals tackled apparently formidable tasks, overcame them and moved on. The group also noticed how they only remembered what and how much had been done when they managed to stop and reflect in this way.

Leadership, conflict and learning

This rapid development was reflected in a growing confidence in certain individuals and in the group as a collective. We had long passed the point where the big events were seen as an end in themselves, and a much wider perspective was evident. This maturing emerged particularly in a clash with the Council's Chief Executive, who had made promises to funders, and was insistent on the timetable for neighbourhood elections in every case – despite the practical difficulties of the facilitators and their needs for flexibility and local adaptations. A series of discussions culminated in a meeting with the entire executive team, who listened carefully to the group, seemed impressed by the facilitators' experiences, and finally agreed it was necessary to be more flexible.

Some months later there was a repetition of this conflict over the timetable for neighbourhood elections, and with the same end result. The executive team wanted to stick to the promised May deadline, but the facilitators argued for a delay to September. At an uncomfortable meeting, the executives were experienced as prescriptive and the facilitators were left visibly angry. May was later dropped in favour of September after various informal negotiations.

These episodes demonstrated the limits of formal leadership in complex, ambiguous situations, where 'learning a way through' seems the only workable course. The facilitators had acquired local knowledge that the executive team did not have, and through their leadership of operations also had an important contribution to make to policy development. In turn, by eventually understanding and accepting this, the executives demonstrated their flexibility and recognized the importance of local knowledge.

Widening circles of inclusivity

For the facilitators, these meetings and discussions with the executive team had the effect of setting neighbourhood events in a yet wider context. With timetables now agreed for neighbourhood elections, the group's work was re-defined again by the – suddenly obvious – need to engage with all the other 'patchworkers'. These neighbourhood-based workers, from various Council departments, partner organizations and the numerous voluntary organizations in the pilot neighbourhoods, now became vital to the handover work of 'mainstreaming' the local priorities as they emerged from the elected neighbourhood committees.

As this new task involved drawing in new people, briefing them and enrolling them into a different way of working, the facilitators' attention also began to shift to the other, non-pilot neighbourhoods in Gladwell. Patchworker events in each neighbourhood were complemented by a two-day 'Action with Communities' event, focusing on Gladwell as a whole, which brought together some 200 residents and workers.

It also became apparent to the facilitators' group that the previous single focus on neighbourhood development had to be married to organization development work in the Council and in the other member organizations of the partnership board. For neighbourhood governance was to be a reality, the partnership organizations had to change the way they did things.

The ambition of this latest vision now appeared in sharp contrast with its chances of success. As the consultants came to the end of their contract, several key members were leaving the facilitators group, with new ones poised to join. Some executive team members were also moving on. The Chief Executive instituted regular meetings with the facilitators group, now with a tighter focus on the implementation of the process in the rest of the neighbourhoods in Gladwell. Business was almost back to usual.

Source: Adapted from Attwood et al. (2003: 39–55)

In search of organizing insight . . .

The Gladwell experience could have appeared in earlier chapters; in Chapter 3 for example, where the action learning adviser's role as accoucheur and designer comes to the fore in setting up the neighbourhood facilitators' set and negotiating its relationship with the Council Chief Executive and the Partnership Board. It could have featured in Chapter 5 to demonstrate the facilitating of organizational learning from the operational work of the set and the policy forums of the Council and the Partnership. The 'middle-ground framework' idea in Chapter 5, which acts as a clutch plate between the levels of learning and action, was developed in Gladwell.

The Gladwell case appears in this chapter because it also illustrates some of the aspirations of a critical action learning in an organizational setting. The unwanted exposure of the seconded Council staff to residents in deprived neighbourhoods left them shorn of their usual protections of office and expert status and feeling anxious, vulnerable and open to learning. They were also exposed in an unusual way to senior officers and policy forums where conflicts and disagreements became apparent. The distribution of powers and the limits to various powers were a normal part of the discussions (although this did not go as far as eliminating 'power games' between some of the facilitators, who all retained their 'day jobs'). Feelings and emotions were often to the fore and publicly expressed. In their meetings with the neighbourhood facilitators, the consultants always felt they were fighting for reflection time, but it was in these pauses in the often frenetic action that the learning from these experiences became apparent and public.

But what might make this critical rather than 'conventional' action learning? Our guess is that, with these learners acquiring insights into the micropolitics of their organizations through their encounters with residents and senior managers, Revans would have seen this as just how action learning should be. The claim to CAL here is that it heightens attention to the power relationships and the emotional aspects of organizational life and how these affect what can be done and what can be learned. In these circumstances, action learning is not a simple and straightforward matter, as is sometimes depicted, of taking one action after another whilst accruing useful learning. This is a much more dangerous and unpredictable process, characterized by ups and downs, upsetting and exciting in turn, revealing glimpses of both oppression and liberation.

Whether this is different from what Revans had imagined we shall never know and it doesn't really matter. What we do know is that this critical perspective has become important and has salience today because it somehow bears upon the pressing and urgent problems of our times.

The contributors to the development of CAL have been concerned to strengthen the power of action learning in organizational settings. The analysis of 'conventional' action learning – that because it is so flexible and adaptable, it is easily and selectively adopted to maintain the status quo – has been demonstrated especially in large corporate settings. The size and power of organizations in the current era may often dwarf that of elected governments and legitimate authorities. Outside these organizations, or existing between them, are many of the 'wicked problems' of communities and societies. If the CAL theorists are right, then action learning needs this sharper edge to address the difficult issues and untaken opportunities of this epoch.

. . . and critical spaces

We have often found it hard to explain exactly what CAL is. But people usually 'get it' once they start to think about it. After a presentation of CAL ideas, some 150 public service managers split up into small groups to reflect. Their feedback was surprisingly unanimous: 'We need spaces where we can analyse and discuss openly what we are doing. We are often required to do things that we disagree with, and this causes great stress for individuals. The opportunity to share this and consider what can be done is vital. This is especially important in difficult times.'

Like any approach based on critical theory, the central value of CAL is that of emancipation; of liberation from restricting attitudes of mind in individuals and from collective mindsets and unquestioning ways that limit or harm ourselves and others. In terms of the outcomes of such critical spaces, the test for their value must be whether they create less oppression and more liberation for all those concerned. It is in this evaluation criterion that the values of critical action learning can perhaps be most clearly distinguished from any more instrumental version that may benefit one party at the expense of others.

Encouraging critical reflection

So how might we actually practise CAL? Some of the examples above point to the centrality of critical reflection in this practice. What is meant by this? Reynolds distinguishes critical reflection from other forms of reflection (see Box 6.5). This four point summary provides a useful checklist against which any action learning set can check its practice. Reflect on your recent reflections; do they meet any of these criteria? And what value would be gained by seeking to meet them all?

Box 6.5 Critical reflection

Critical reflection is distinguished by:

1   being concerned with questioning assumptions
2   having a social rather than an individual focus
3   paying particular attention to the analysis of power relations
4   being concerned with emancipation

Source: Adapted from Reynolds (1998)

Critical action learning in a set

Box 6.6 gives an example from a recent action learning set.

Box 6.6 Critical reflection in action

Josie came to the action learning set for set advisers in despair: 'I rarely use the word hate but I do really hate the set I am working with. They are a group of newly qualified staff and the action learning set is supposed to be supporting them but this feeling of hate and dread I feel is not supporting anybody.'

Colleague: 'Tell us more about the set.'

Josie: 'Well there are five altogether – three white male and two black female. The men just dominate the process and me, constantly putting me down and the service – the women just stay silent – the set meeting gets into a destructive cycle and I go away feeling angry.'

The set continued to explore how Josie might focus the group more positively then:

Colleague: 'I remember you saying that the set is composed of three white male and with you three black females and I am wondering to what extent what is happening in the set is represented in the wider organization.'

Josie: 'Yes – to a certain extent is does. All the managers are white men and as a senior team leader I know that I am intimidated, even repressed by the management team and that makes me angry and frustrated. The insight for me is that I have never thought of the set representing the organization in this way.'

Colleague: 'OK then can I then push you a bit further – are you modelling this repression as a norm to the two newly qualified black women in the set?'

Josie: 'What you are saying is am I perpetuating an organizational culture that makes me unhappy? So in the set I am 'hating' not three members but what those members represent to me and black women in the organization and at the same time encouraging by my behaviour the two black women to see this as normal.'

The set continued to explore this new evolving issue . . .

This encounter could have stopped with exploring ways in which Josie could focus the group more positively and feel more positive herself about her role as facilitator. Our view is that this became CAL when her attention was drawn to the wider context of the organizational structure and culture then focusing back down to her own role in perpetuating that culture not just herself but for others. In a subsequent meeting Josie reported the feeling of liberation and how this insight had allowed her to work with the set encouraging set members to think more critically about the set as a micro organization. This heightened awareness of the political and cultural aspects of organizations for the set can be very powerful, even dangerous. In this case the set had been meeting for some time and there was a powerful sense of trust between colleagues – is this an essential ingredient for CAL?

In the case study CAL evolved naturally in the meeting, however, here is an activity to try in a set to encourage critical thinking (Box 6.7):

Box 6.7 Activity 1: Different voices

In an action learning set, where the members know and trust each other well, use the following activity to practise and strengthen the habits of critical thinking from independent standpoints.

When one member is discussing a course of action that may be controversial, stop the discussion and introduce this ten-minute activity:

1 Brainstorm a list of different standpoints from which critical voices of any course of action could come. Make up a list to match the number in the set. For example:

Manager		Parent
Chief Executive		Teacher
Main supplier	OR	Neighbour
Customer		Police
Local politician		Child
Environmental campaigner		Child psychologist

2   Write each of these 'voices' on a card and place them face down on the table.
3   Have members draw random cards in turn and speak from these positions about the proposed course of action.
4   When all voices have been heard, ask the proposer of the action what they have heard.

Is there anything new here?
How will what they have heard affect what they might do next?

The set could move on to consider the outcome of this activity in terms of Reynold's four criteria (Box 6.5). They may conclude that they have certainly achieved criteria 1: *questioning assumptions*, but what about 2, 3 and 4?

The achievement of these three probably requires more than ordinary criticality, and may need a prompt from CST – critical social theory – perhaps the hint that organizations and societies tend to be organized in ways that disguise inequities or make them appear normal or natural. Much effort is often made via the media and other forms of cultural dissemination to maintain this 'normality'.

The application of such ideas in action learning sets, might enable participants, in Burgoyne and Reynolds' words (1997: 1), to distinguish between:

- effective practice
- reflective practice
  and
- critically reflective practice.

CRP: critically reflective practice

What does this look like? According to Brookfield (2011) the overall purpose of CRP is to develop political acumen and to learn how organizations function as political systems. Although this can again be read as an extension of Revans' thoughts about micropolitics, this is now developed as a practice in itself, the skills in which can be considered in some more detail (Box 6.8).

Box 6.8 CRP

A critically reflective practice aims to:

- unearth power dynamics and how power flows round communities, organizations and societies;
- understand how power is used responsively, or abused, and how it is collectively exercised;
- uncover ideological manipulation and understand how ideology is embedded in micro-actions and everyday decisions;
- understand how we collude in our own marginalization; as for example when we behave in ways that bind us damagingly to positions or decisions – 'killing you softly';
- recognize how the system manages and sees off challenges, for example by 'Repressive Tolerance' (Marcuse) where what presents itself as a democratic tolerance of ALL viewpoints, effectively 'flattens conversation', encourages 'intellectual tourism' and perpetuates dominance of the mainstream.

Source: Author's notes on Brookfield (2011)

There is much food for thought – and action – here. Consider the times you have been in compromised situations: what was your part in arriving there? Consider perhaps, as a manager, the times you have 'welcomed all views' – and breathed a sigh of relief when critical voices were lost in the variety.

Whilst there is no necessary 'administrative evil' implied here, such interpersonal practices are commonplace in organizations and are used perhaps largely unconsciously to achieve short-term goals. None of us – except perhaps for the heroic critically reflective and reflexive practitioner, is immune to them.

Box 6.9 offers another practice activity to strengthen the CRP muscles. In Activity 1, action learning members develop their awareness of wider perspectives, but this is more of an ordinary criticality which does not necessarily reach the level of a social critique. In Activity 2 the alternative

stances are based on different value positions which are likely to be fundamentally critical of any existing state of affairs.

Box 6.9 Activity 2: Alternative stances

This activity can be done via email between the members of an action
learning set. It works better in a virtual rather than a face-to-face (f2f)
setting because it gives each person some time to think and perhaps to
read up on their stance.

Choose a problem situation from one of the members that seems
especially complex or confusing. Perhaps a set member has been put a
complicated or 'political' situation or perhaps they are faced with a
seemingly impossible dilemma.

1   The person concerned with the difficult situation first emails their
    colleagues with brief description of the situation facing them.
    At the foot of this description the situation owner should add
    the following stances:

    • Marxist
    • feminist
    • environmentalist
    • free market economist
    • NIMBY (not in my back yard)
    • anti-colonial campaigner

    and then allocate each of their fellow set members to a different
    stance.
2   Each member then responds to the email *from the allocated
    stance* within an agreed time frame; say within one week, or in
    time for the next meeting.
    NB Members can do any research they wish to work out their
    stance and the likely position to be taken on the issue. The aim
    is to work from the value position of that stance to propose an
    analysis and suggestions for action.
3   When all the stances have been posted, the person who initiated
    the exchange should then summarize the insights they have
    gained from the process together with any new questions.
4   If possible, a f2f meeting is probably best suited to digesting the
    outcomes of this activity and especially with helping the person
    with their next steps.

The stances activity is likely to push any set beyond the questioning assumptions of 'ordinary criticality' into a more social critique of how power works to enable some things and prevent others. The different ideological stances move beyond the differences of perceptions between say, a customer and a supplier, who inhabit similar worlds, to radically different worldview of how things might be. What next?

Both these activities, Boxes 6.7 and 6.9, are what Kelly called loosening rather than tightening exercises (Banister and Fransella 1971: 33–4) – that is to say they open you up, but do not necessarily tell you what to do next. Before considering this tricky question, the following is by way of a health warning, also from Stephen Brookfield who provided the CRP skills in Box 6.8.

Critical thinking: the dark side

From an analysis of autobiographical accounts of 'critical thinking episodes', Brookfield (1994) found that, whilst questioning assumptions, adopting alternative perspectives and so on could be experienced as very liberating and even lead to what he calls 'transformative breakthroughs', they could also produce some very negative reactions and feelings.

Alert readers may have already spotted that critical thinking can get you into trouble. Here's how (Box 6.10):

Box 6.10 Critical thinking: the dark side

Brookfield's research showed that people who engaged in critical thinking often suffered from the following:

- Feelings of 'impostorship' – doubting one's worthiness to question the ideas of eminent people
- 'Lost innocence' – consequent upon the questioning of one's own personal taken-for-granted ideas
- Despair at the implications of taking a radical analysis of their professional context
- 'Cultural suicide' in encountering other people's hostility at their critical questioning of accepted practices

Source: Adapted from Brookfield (1994)

Then why bother? Well, simply because this is part of the territory of addressing significant issues. As Revans always pointed out, action learning carries a 'risk imperative': 'These attacks, whether upon problems or opportunities, must carry a significant risk of penalty for failure' (2011: 6).

It is the risk involved which makes for the significance of the learning; no risk, no significant learning. It is for this reason that Revans often referred to set members as 'comrades in adversity' because he knew that action learners – and surely this applies even more so to critical action learners – need all the help they can get. Working in sets and building support networks in the wider system are not optional extras but essential to supporting this risky work.

Action learners as tempered radicals

The aim of the last part of this chapter has been to encourage people to try out CAL, on the basis that it might be a necessary strengthening of the action learning impulse for the intractable issues of our times. There may even have been a hint or two in these pages that the answer may be found here to the question: how do you do CAL? Hopefully some useful disciplines have been illustrated and some seeds have been sown. There is one last idea that might also be helpful: the notion of the action learner as tempered radical (Attwood 2007).

Tempered radicals (Myerson and Scully 1995; Myerson 2003) are people who identify with and are committed to their organizations, but are simultaneously committed to a cause, community or ideology which differs fundamentally from the dominant culture of their organizations. They are 'people who want to succeed in their organizations yet want to live by their values or identities, even if they are somehow at odds with the dominant culture of their organizations . . .

Tempered radicals want to fit in and they want to retain what makes them different. They want to rock the boat, and they want to stay in it' (Myerson 2003: xi).

These people are radicals who are not afraid to challenge the status quo, but they are also tempered and toughened by their experiences of previous battles against what they see as injustices and inefficiencies. The tempered radical position is one of being on the edge, standing both in and outside the organization as the basis for judgements and actions. As Myerson says, this ambivalent stance creates a number of special challenges and opportunities.

Conclusion

A critical practice of action learning borrows from critical social theory to sharpen the edge of Revans' idea in an era where notions about organization and organizing have become less taken for granted and more plural and contested. Action learning can benefit from critical theory, but rejects any assumed superiority on the part of theory and theorists over practice and practitioners. The value of critical thinking is acknowledged but only if this is offered in the spirit of peer inquiry and in the context of a mutual striving for useful action and practical accomplishment. The understanding is important, but it is only part of the journey to useful action and learning.

This chapter includes some activities and ideas for developing critical thinking and critical reflection, which are helpful in pursuing a course of critical action learning. They provide the means to distinguish between effective practice, reflective practice and critically reflective practice. This practice however must be brought out of the set and into action in wider systems. As Reynolds and Vince put it: 'Do ideas brought into action-based discussions help to question existing practices, structures and associated power relations within the organization?' (2004: 453).

A critical practice of action learning not only questions existing practices, structures and associated power relations, but also aims to change them for the better. A big ask.

My practice notes 6

Critical action learning

Make some notes on this aspect of the action learning adviser's role as it relates to your current practice. You may want to consider such questions as:

- *Am I convinced by the case for CAL?*

- *Is CAL part of what I do now? Should it be?*

- *Which aspect of this stance attracts me – and what doesn't?*

- *Which critical skills would I like to acquire?*

What are my thoughts about Vince's notion 'Organizing Insight'? What does it add to Revans' Questioning Insight'?

How can I encourage critically reflective practice?

What can be done about the dark side of critical thinking?

How do I feel about the notion of action learners as tempered radicals?

Reflection on *My practice notes 6*:

Reading through what I have just written on these aspects of Critical Action Learning, what does it say about my practice?

7 An action learning way of working

Chapter overview

This chapter revisits the values proposed by Revans in examining the purpose of action learning. The implications of management development as a moral business are considered especially in relation to the question: what difference are we making?

This discussion prefaces an exploration of the application of action learning to developing particular forms of organizing including facilitative leadership, partnership and networks. These are illustrated with case studies and examples from practice which show that action learning can make a difference in terms of 'social' or 'relational capital', that is in terms of the quality of relationships between people.

It is argued that the purpose, values and methods of action learning lend themselves to some particular needs of the time and towards a vision for organizing where action learning is seen as a part of normal work. This is a long-term venture, but the ambitious action learning adviser is invited to see themselves as contributing to a more effective and fulfilling way of working and organizing. The chapter ends with the suggestion that this can be done via the triple practices of facilitative leadership, network organizing and an action learning way of working.

This chapter contains:

- Introduction
- The purpose of action learning
- Facilitative leadership
- Developing partnership
- Creating knowledge communities
- Network organizing
- Organizing for the needs of the time
- My practice notes 7

Introduction

In Chapter 5, we looked at the action learning adviser's role as a facilitator of organizational learning. Here the adviser is seeking to encourage the spreading of learning from the action learning sets into the wider organization, community or system. As we noted in that chapter, any action learning adviser working on these aspects soon realizes that some kinds of learning and knowledge have the potential to be useful beyond the boundaries of any individual system, organization, profession or community.

This is especially true of *process* knowledge; that is knowledge of how to do things. The knowledge which has most potential to be widely diffused are the particular ways of learning and working which are produced in, and are characteristic of, action learning. Properly understood, action learning can be seen as a working process which creates new webs of connection and ways of organizing between people.

In this chapter we encourage action learning practitioners to revisit their purpose in engaging with action learning in the context of the invisible and intangible experiences of individuals in an organization that collectively contribute to the shared understanding of the way the organization works. This understanding includes the interconnections that have been developed among individuals both within and without the organizational boundaries and how through the lens of action learning these interconnections can be explored to develop knowledge communities, networked organizing and partnership working.

Before moving into this wider world of organizing we take another look at the purpose of action learning and its characteristic values. As we have seen action learning has many varieties of practice and will invent many more, but what holds these practitioners together in a practice community, is their striving to realize certain values of relationship, learning and organizing.

The purpose of action learning

> All meaningful knowledge is for the sake of action, and all meaningful
> action is for the sake of friendship.
>
> Macmurray quoted by Revans (2011:
> Frontispiece – *Some Eminent Precursors*)

A glance at any of Revans' writings will reveal that he did not see his action learning as a narrow philosophy. Together with the eminent precursors that he likes to quote, he not only wants to improve the way organizations work, but by 'Helping each other to help the helpless' (1982: 467–92), to make the world a better place.

Revans' particular contribution is to the field of management and organization, but if his ambitions had been limited to devising a new method for management development, then action learning would long ago have faded from sight. Whilst management and organization development are the abiding focus, the action learning idea can offer a wider perspective on how to live, work and learn together.

Perhaps it is this broader purpose and underlying values of action learning that bind together the community of practice more than any agreement on method or technique. Action learning practitioners come in a great variety, and their individual practices can differ markedly, but can be equally authentic if there is broad agreement on values.

Management as a moral business

For Revans, management is at heart a moral business, concerned with right and wrong choices and with their implications for human development. He could be both scathing and despairing when action learning was reduced to technique or formula, and would respond, as previously noted, with great lists of what action learning is *not* (2011: 77–93), but also by insisting that action learning is not new, but involves the fresh interpretation of old and profound ideas (2011: viii):

> It is a small thing to find historical references to learning by doing, or to discharging a duty towards belief by testing its validity in action: *it is something greater to identify the basic ideas of action learning as the essence of a universal movement, cultural, political or religious.*
>
> (1982: 532, our emphasis)

He is struck by the similarity between action learning and Buddhist ideas, and quotes the four truths about suffering: what suffering is, how it is caused, how it may be stopped, and the fourth – 'that awakens the greatest interest in the student of action learning: "This is the path leading to the cessation of suffering – this I have declared"' (1982: 538). We don't usually talk about suffering in the managerial world, where even Revans' word 'problem' can cause problems, and we must talk instead of tasks, goals, targets and 'challenges'. Nonetheless, it is hard to miss Revans' essentially humanistic motivation alongside his pragmatic concerns for improvement. In his most formal exposition of action learning as a model of strategic action, 'Managerial values' form the very first part of system alpha (1971: 28, 34–5).

Action learning's characteristic assumptions

We noted some of these values in Chapter 1; they form the basis for assessing whether we are doing it right and for whether what is being practised is authentic action learning. To get the sense of these, you can't do better than to reflect upon the 15 short pages of the ABC (2011: 1–15), where Revans lists 20 characteristic assumptions of action learning. These have to be interpreted in practice, and each of us has to understand what these mean for us and how they can be put into practice. For example, Box 7.1 gives a short-list selection.

Box 7.1 A short list of action learning values

- The purpose of action learning is to improve things (for oneself and for others).
- Action learning is only for volunteers.
- It requires the tackling of important organizational or social problems or opportunities.
- Honest and courageous attempts to address difficult problems lead to significant learning.
- Such work cannot be done alone and needs help from other people.
- The set – or small group of trusted peers with equal voice – is vital.
- Fresh questions have particular value.
- Any learning from action should be shared with wider circles beyond the set.

Are we doing it right?

Any practitioner needs some such list in mind, for otherwise how do we know whether we are doing it right? For example, taking the second value in Box 7.1, an early question to any new client could be: 'How will people volunteer for this programme or venture?', a question that can be asked in a number of ways (and it is very interesting to hear how other people ask it; and of course, whether they do). But this alone might not be enough to uphold the volunteering principle, and it is often necessary to ask a follow-up: 'How is it possible for a person to say no to this programme (without loss of face, favour etc.)?' and this is the one which might prove most uncomfortable for the honest client, who may struggle to give a satisfactory answer. Every practitioner must decide how much they will risk questions like this; Chapter 3 has an example of David Casey asking a client the same question over a period of eight months. Many of us may not push it this far, and it may be a question of designing projects so that the volunteering ideal is more, rather than less, possible.

How can this be done? Though there is no definitive answer here beyond consulting the set, considerable efforts have been made by some practitioners to establish measurable standards.

Critical markers, gold standards, ethical frameworks and authentic action learning

Understanding Revans' emancipatory intent, and concerned that some of what is called 'action learning' may fall short of his values, some practitioners have tackled the authentification problem by determining some quality control criteria.

Willis lists 23 'critical markers' of a 'Revans' Gold Standard', which she employs in inspecting a variety of US cases, concluding that: 'Unfortunately they do not furnish strong, convincing evidence that Revans' theory-intact is being practiced anywhere in US organisations' (2004: 25). On the basis of the critical markers, she constructs a useful spectrum of practice which is 'more like action learning' to that which is 'less like action learning' (Figure 7.1). Willis points out that practitioners who are at the 'more like' end are likely to have had some grounding in adult or progressive education or organization development rather than those whose background is in 'performance technology concepts' 'step-wise learning procedures' and 'hierarchical systems' (2004: 25–6).

Building upon Willis, Johnson (2010) takes a 'consumer protection' perspective in his 20 item ethical framework for 'authentic' action learning in higher education settings. Coughlan and Coghlan address themselves to the question of action learning research, and in order to differentiate this from other forms of research, suggest four main dimensions for assessing quality (2011: 175). Whilst this is useful work, there is always a danger in such codification of losing the simplicity which Revans strove for. As he once said to a nurse who exclaimed in great delight that she had

Figure 7.1 A spectrum of authentic action learning
Source: After Willis (2004)

at last understood action learning: 'Very good, but now what are you going to do about it?'

What difference are we making?

A list of values or criteria may help to judge what difference we are making, in providing a basis for evaluation and for assessing progress. We talked about evaluation in Chapter 3 and gave an illustration of how to evaluate the work of the set, but the fundamental evaluation questions for action learning are always the same (Box 7.2).

Box 7.2 What difference are we making?

- Are difficult problems being addressed?
- Are ideas being tested in action?
- What evidence is there of learning, in terms of:

    (i)   personal development?
    (ii) learning in the set as a collective?
    (iii) organizational learning?

These simple questions can be used at several levels. They can operate as a rule of thumb to check any project's authenticity; or at a deeper level they may demand extensive efforts at evaluation. They can also be widely applied in any sphere of human functioning – in families, groups, neighbourhoods, organizations or societies.

With the purpose and values in mind, what is the different way of working that action learning offers? What does it mean to work with this idea in the contexts of leadership, partnership and organizing?

Facilitative leadership

> *The problem is the domain of the leader; unlike the puzzle, it is charged with unanswerable questions as well as unformulatable ones.*
> (Revans 1982: 712)

As recently as 1965, 'management' was still widely called 'industrial administration' (Revans 1980: 193) and 'leadership' only concerned those at the very top of the shop. Yet, leadership is the obvious locus of Revans' concern with problems rather than puzzles, and also an obvious starting point for action learning in any system. Today, action learning is perhaps most commonly found in organizational leadership programmes, where it usually has a personal development and 'own job' focus.

We are interested in a wider conception of leadership than is sometimes offered on those programmes; wider both in terms of leadership in any social system and particularly in the idea of leadership as a collective capacity or as a culture. A widespread capacity for leadership can develop where people are encouraged to voice their ideas and try them out in working with colleagues on organizational problems. This is what Raelin (2003) has called the 'leaderful' organization (see Box 7.3).

Box 7.3 A leaderful organization?

A company with only one leader is short of leadership.
Gerald Egan

At Digital Equipment in Burlington, Vermont, action learning was seen as an important component of leadership development (Adams and Dixon 1997). As part of a nine month programme for managers and supervisors entitled 'World Class Leadership', action learning sets met weekly to:

- learn data-driven problem-solving skills;
- discover and change 'taken-for-granted' rules that impede effective group problem solving;
- develop the ability to re-frame problems and situations;
- develop high performance teams;
- learn coaching, consultation and project management skills;
- resolve business issues.

Adams and Dixon suggest that a regular commitment to action learning over time produced a great number of benefits for Digital, which were experienced at personal, team and organizational levels.

Of particular interest here is how such a programme might develop. Ideas about leadership have proliferated in recent years; old ideas of command and charisma are out of fashion, collaborative and 'distributed' models are in, yet the hierarchical and control impulses remain a deeply ingrained 'default' position. But whilst we may often resort to this basic impulse, it doesn't usually deliver much in terms of leadership.

A survey of 90,000 workers in 18 countries concluded that only 21 per cent were engaged in their work to the extent that 'they would go the extra mile'; whilst almost twice as many reported themselves as mostly or entirely disengaged (Hamel 2012). The standard response sort of data is that it is a cultural problem – most employees are disengaged because their managers are indifferent and don't care about them – and therefore the answer is for leaders and managers to practise engagement strategies and create cultures fit for aspiring and creative employees. Action learning might be a good way to do this.

On the basis of leadership development work in the creative and cultural industries sector, Venner (2009) describes how action learning helps to develop the quality of relationships that keep people engaged, challenged and continuing to learn: 'It teaches you to facilitate your peers as they tackle complex organisational challenges. These skills are directly transferable to your board, team, freelance enterprise, collaborative partnership and organisation, whatever your leadership role' (Venner 2009: 5). Venner calls this 'facilitative leadership', and, according to the participants on such programmes, it involves a particular set of skills (Pedler 2011):

- attending – focusing attention;
- listening – listening to and understanding what others have to say rather than imposing own views;
- questioning – asking good and critical questions which surface underlying issues and lead to creative outcomes;
- reflecting – ability to think through and make sense both before and after taking action;
- learning – learning new skills, learning from group situations and generally from reflecting on experience;
- giving fewer solutions – 'unlearning the compulsion to offer solutions'.

Unsurprisingly perhaps, these are also action learning skills. This skills set offers an alternative view on leadership in which 'unlearning the compulsion to offer solutions' is especially striking.

Facilitative leadership is a nice idea, but the problem of disengagement and poorly performing organizations may not be just be cultural. Bossy bosses and callous corporate cultures must surely turn people off, but there could also be a structural problem. Are organizational blueprints based on hierarchy, with their asymmetric reward systems and bureaucratic understrappings, increasingly unfit for purpose?

Developing partnership

As facilitative leadership, action learning encourages collaboration, peer learning and getting things done, and so can work very well in bringing people together to create partnerships. Box 7.4 describes a case where several organizations came together around a common concern.

Box 7.4 A buyer/supplier collaboration

After a number of meetings and discussions, an action learning programme was established in a UK region between an NHS Foundation Trust, two NHS suppliers of health products and a pharmaceutical company. The participants were doctors, managers and other health professionals and senior sales and logistics people from the three suppliers. The overall purpose was to improve the quality and efficiency of supplies and the supply chain.

Whilst individual participants agreed projects with their own sponsors, strong guidelines for project selection were agreed by a steering group:

'Projects should:

- focus on a problem – to which there is no known solution – rather than a puzzle for which a solution is more readily apparent;
- have the potential to improve relationships between participating organizations;
- support the personal development of individual participants and be part of their personal development plans;
- encourage participants to venture beyond the "walls" of their own organizations.'

Of course, each organization had different interests, as well as some which were shared. The NHS purchasing managers wanted to save money, whilst the suppliers wanted to sell more goods and services. Each took a risk in sharing information and knowledge which could be of financial value to the other. These risks were knowingly taken in the hope of better long-term collaboration, but they were risks nonetheless.

In this case the purpose was a specific and temporary one: to learn about different needs and systems, and to sort out what had become untidy supply arrangements. There was no intention of creating a long-term relationship; it would have been improper for the Trust to have what could be seen as a 'sweetheart deal' with any supplier, and the suppliers were in competition with each other.

Social capital

Nonetheless, when relationships are formed between people and between groups of people, these can endure, often beyond the lives of the organizations that employed them at the time. In another case, a local authority set up some action learning sets with groups of people drawn from adult social services, community nurses and care home owners. This was in the early 1990s, but it is still apparently easier and quicker to get people in, and out of, care in this part of the county, than it is in neighbouring parts.

The creation of social capital is an exciting potential of action learning (Pedler and Attwood 2011). Each time someone helps another out, this produces more social capital, which adds to a fund of goodwill based on trusting relationships, from which all partners can draw to help them get their work done. Because of the trust, people communicate more fully, and are prepared to go that extra mile for each other. Whilst this is not rocket science, neither does it come about overnight, or by accident.

In the example in Box 7.5, a UK City Council established a partnership group with other agencies to try and change the relationships between officers and residents in their neighbourhoods.

Box 7.5 Neighbourhood partnerships

A partnership group in a city of some 400,000 people established neighbourhood action learning groups of local residents and officers from the various agencies and departments. The aim was to change the relationships between officials from local government, education, health, police, probation and other professionals with local residents. Whilst all the agencies are committed to serving the local people, over time a big gap had appeared between officers' decisions and local needs, especially in the more deprived neighbourhoods.

Action learning sets were introduced as a new way of meeting together. For most officers, the normal way of meeting is the committee, with formal procedures, agendas, minutes, and an 'only speak to your particular item' culture. The few residents who attend such committees usually have little to say. In the action learning forums, 'air-time' was equally shared and everyone spoke in turn – about who they were, what they did and what they were trying to do. People were encouraged to question each other to find new information and to offer help where they could. At the end of each meeting, people 'checked out' and said what they would do before the next meeting.

Over a year or so, the action learning sets produced several outcomes including a plan for each neighbourhood, with agreed priorities, and also new agreements about how the various professional agencies should work together. Another outcome was new relationships between people – between officers and residents, officers and officers, and residents and residents. At a review session people said:

- I've met a lot of new people, nice people, who I would not have met before.
- I use this group to discuss problems, to get it straight before I go to committee and when I get there I am much clearer about what is needed.
- I call up people between meetings and they give me contacts and networks which I would never have known about.
- All sorts of connections have resulted from these meetings which have worked in somewhat mysterious but helpful ways.

The process was not without difficulties. It was hard to find resident volunteers in some neighbourhoods. The action learning process was unfamiliar and took time to develop. There were also awkward questions: some volunteers seemed to represent their own special interests rather than those of the neighbourhood; and whilst officers got paid whilst attending sessions, residents only got travel expenses. Over time the initiative gradually ran out of steam, more in some areas than in others, but the achievements were real enough: new neighbourhood plans, new ways of meeting, and at best a genuine sense of excitement and joint endeavour.

Creating knowledge communities

Go to the ant, thou sluggard, consider her ways and be wise: which, having no guide, overseer, or ruler, provideth her meat in the summer and gathereth her food in the harvest.

Proverbs 6 (6–8)

Whilst we don't know how they do it, ants have long been a model of how to organize. We know that each ant works autonomously, and yet somehow collaboratively, to achieve community goals. There seems to be no King ants, but anthills are mainly composed of females. Perhaps that's a clue?

Because action learning promotes partnership, facilitative leadership and social capital, it can also work with less structured forms of organizing such as networks and communities of practice. As we saw in Chapter 5, these are increasingly important for knowledge workers and professionals of all kinds. They form around shared interests and learning needs, and the work of building partnership and collaboration becomes the actual organizing itself. The peer relationships which characterize these communities and networks make them particularly suited to action learning sets, which can bring people together and act as building blocks (Box 7.6).

Box 7.6 Building knowledge communities

Sets can be formed in many ways in knowledge communities and networks. People can be invited to join in sets by:

- inviting any work community – such as those just completing a management development programme – to form groups of their own volition and offering them logistical support and facilitation if needed;
- bringing together people with similar problems or challenges but from different work situations or sectors;
- developing an 'oversight' group with members from different work teams;
- inviting people to tackle a specific theme or problem area for the organization;
- asking for volunteers to start opening up a new area of activity in which the company wishes to develop new knowledge;
- starting some virtual action learning by inviting any number of people to work on an organizational issue online;
- creating a group to establish some new cultural forms for the organization, for example, changing the typical forms of meeting or working.

Professional networks usually operate on such principles as:

- shared purposes and goals;
- learning exchanges;
- relationships of sharing, exchange and influencing;
- self-initiation and self-organizing rather than being managed;
- status and recognition based on knowledge, expertise and connectedness not hierarchical position.

This way of working places a premium upon social or 'relational capital' (Cross and Parker 2004: 131–2). If you are an engineer or financial director, an HR specialist or a scientist, where are you likely to find your new knowledge? Performing well as a professional increasingly means being well connected to professional bodies and forums where the latest knowledge and 'best practices' are likely to be found.

Network organizing

> *No company can go it alone.*
>
> Doz and Hamel 1998: ix

Network organizing is increasingly common in the more formal world of work, via partnerships, strategic alliances, joint ventures, supply chains, research and development collaborations and training consortia. There is a long-term epochal shift taking place here which can be described as moving from structures of control towards structures of connection (Figure 7.2).

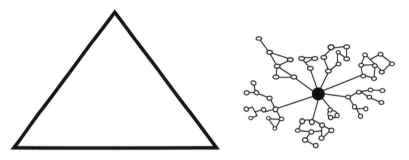

Figure 7.2 Structures of control and structures of connection

Network structures are essential to certain sorts of work, from 'Third Sector' organizations such as the Royal National Lifeboat Institution to Age UK, which rely on the cooperation of many thousands of volunteers and the collaboration of many private and public organizations. Some of the most difficult challenges in life seem to involve network organizing. Mountain Rescue is an interesting case; it can save your life but only if complex collaborations are achieved. In the UK Peak District the following have to work well together to achieve success:

- seven all-volunteer Mountain Rescue Teams (MRTs) who undergo considerable and regular training and practice sessions, and manage resources include rescue equipment, Landrovers and search and rescue dogs (which take two years to train for working lives of perhaps five to seven years);

- three Air Ambulance services with helicopters which are charities, 30 per cent funded by the NHS;
- four NHS Ambulance Trusts with ambulances and paramedics;
- various NHS Trusts and trauma centres in Sheffield, Manchester, Staffordshire, Nottingham and Derby and other smaller towns, with medical and nursing specialists and care facilities.

All these partners have different resources, motivations, affiliations, organizational rules and management and governance structures. Leadership shifts around from one MRT to another as negotiations on vital matters such as the responsibility for an injured person and the use of medical supplies are decided locally, and may conflict with single organizational rules.

In the NHS itself, networks are increasingly essential for delivering quality services. Better cancer care for example; ensuring equality of access to care requires new ways of working by the big teaching hospitals and tertiary centres who must learn to share their expertise and resources with local hospitals. In the 22 UK Trauma Networks, lives are saved when ambulance drivers learn to pass their 'home' hospitals and go immediately to the appropriate specialist unit.

The need to work in this networked way may seem so obvious as to need no further explanation, but there is still much to do. Much organizing is still based on a single hierarchical structure, because this is held to be the best form for accounting for profit or cost or quality. But certainly not for learning, nor for other aspects of effectiveness. Accountability is simpler and easier to do in isolated units, but at what cost? It is said for example, that in Zambia alone there are over 1600 foreign NGOs with healthcare missions, often competing with one another. The benefits of collaboration may be obvious, but it's not how we do things (yet).

This creates plenty of opportunities for the action learning adviser as network organizer. Action learning can be designed to:

- develop and strengthen relationships between people in the same or different functions, departments or organizations;
- build informal networks across operational units;
- develop skills in leadership, collaborative working and interpersonal communication;
- impact on the organizational culture in beneficial ways as we saw in the Irish Health Board.

All these processes can be seen at work in the case example in Box 7.7. Here the requirement for change is a compelling one, brought about by a crisis in the existing operating system which gives the new senior managers the freedom to create the sort of learning organization they want to bring about. Action learning is consciously used here to develop network learning across the organization.

Box 7.7 The hospital as a learning network

In the mid-1990s, a scandal in an Austrian city hospital exposed corrupt practices by some senior managers and professionals. The hospital employed some 2000 people, including 120 managers, and is accountable to the City Council. After much investigation and thought, a new top management team was installed and set out to establish a new direction and mission for the hospital. The new top managers participated in an intensive management course and promoted a mood of 'We want to develop and perform on a high level with integrity', which they saw as already existing among many employees.

The development and change process

A survey conducted among hospital employees revealed a long list of challenges and problems, including:

- poor patient relationships including lack of staff friendliness, increasing demands from patients and a growing complexity of treatments;
- dissatisfaction and rudeness among doctors and low discipline from some who participated in management;
- severe communication blocks between administration, doctors and nurses;
- little identification with the organization as a whole by staff, with much anonymity and isolation, including 'forgotten groups';
- overcentralization and lack of transparency; seemingly endless decision processes, and frustration about what was felt as a very high degree of formality;
- fighting and blaming as predominant ways of conflict handling;
- not enough support from superiors with too little or no feedback in regard of actions and initiatives.

Yet, it was also noted that there was much vitality amongst the staff who also made many proposals for improvement.

Management development through action learning

As part of the renewal process, a management development programme was designed to integrate learning and project work to bring about necessary changes and to encourage learning partnerships and interdisciplinary cooperation among staff.

In cohorts of 20, all 120 managers participated in six two-and-a-half day conferences over a year, with inputs of knowledge and skills as both required and requested. Each manager also chose an action learning project, with a client (mostly heads of departments) and a sponsor (mostly high-ranking managers) and was made personally responsible for negotiating the action and the results of this project. Projects were chosen from a long list of strategic issues drawn up by management and participants, and included:

* optimization of patient routing;
* patient transport within the hospital;
* project to gain feedback from the patients;
* introduction for doctors in training;
* building adaptations for disabled persons;
* developing a new mission for the nursing school;
* employee satisfaction surveys;
* remobilization of older patients;
* organization of day care;
* telephone behaviours;
* communication between pharmacy and other departments;
* organizational consequences of the new financial arrangements;
* waste reduction strategies.

The action learning groups of about six people met for ten whole day meetings over a year. Participants met with their clients to negotiate the assignment and monitor the progress made, and with personal sponsors to help with 'helicopter views' and political support. All parties are expected to learn from these meetings and to initiate improvements on the basis of their experiences.

Personal and organizational benefits

Over several years these activities promoted a culture of learning from work experience which provoked more open communication and cooperation between professional groups. Striking successes were achieved by dozens of participants who experienced that their initiatives were well honoured and recognized. As well as these many practical outcomes, the programme also led to increases in personal competence and a broadening of attitudes. Typical remarks were:

- 'Questioning is becoming a habit for me' (nurse)
- 'I realize that we are looking more at the broader context and are thinking less fragmentarily' (medical department head)
- 'We don't get lost so often in our discussions: the clarified objectives keep us on track' (head nurse)

At group and department levels, the new rules of behaviour practised in the learning sets is changing the way the hospital staff work together:

- 'I now experience a lot of leeway – I had not expected we would gain so much liberty of action out of this programme' (head of purchasing)
- 'The "owner principle" (owner of the meeting; owner of an agenda-item, owner of an assignment) helps us to overcome the usual unclear arrangements' (junior doctor)
- 'I am happy that I can get valid information now so quickly – the network relations I got out of my own set and from other sets are a great help' (hospital technician)
- 'The network relations which develop between members of sets contribute a lot to conflict prevention' (medical head of department)
- 'I look forward to our collegial consulting sessions where we coach each other – each time I get glimpses of new worlds from the working situations of colleagues from other professions' (manager)

The self-organization of learning groups also caught on well. After half a year of practice 'veteran' learning sets invited members of later sets to share findings about 'how to craft learning group sessions'. Participants whose entrepreneurial attitudes had been activated by the rhythms of acting and learning in the sets were much better equipped to cope with uncertainties and rapid changes. The regular conferences created common perspective and a structure of network learning through the feedback loops from implementation of the many projects. In these ways, participants learned that they could make effective contributions within a structure that they had co-determined.

The challenge is to shape the future of the hospital even more consciously and vigorously by making network learning core to the operating conditions of the organization.

Source: Adapted with permission from
Donnenberg (2011: 297–312)

Network learning

As in the Irish example from Chapter 5, this Austrian case shows that a culture of network learning is not brought about overnight, but has to be sustained, perhaps over several years. This is greatly helped by continuity in the senior leadership team.

Can these sorts of changes, in cultures, structures and processes, be done more quickly? In all the cases in this book, the improvements in performance and operations take time to be conceived, negotiated, experimented with and proved. The learning from these innovations also emerges over time. As noted in Chapter 3, the commissioning of research or evaluation projects can be very helpful for this learning because they can create the means and the legitimacy for collective reflection. This headroom for learning space is usually impossible to find in organizations driven by short-term performance. Here action dominates, but the absence of any learning space means that these actions tend to repeat themselves, rightly sometimes perhaps, but eventually wrongly.

In the organizational world, it is unusual to have the benefit of a long period for reflection, but in the Austrian hospital case we are fortunate to have the action learning adviser's reflections on the outcomes some 15 years after the start of the work (Box 7.8).

Box 7.8 Donnenberg on network learning

What do we learn from 'The Hospital as a Learning Network' case? There are several points to make about the right conditions for learning, innovation and network working:

1 *Individualistic learning can be detrimental to connectivity* Within the fragmented organization of a hospital with its many subcultures there is a great need for integrating the many efforts to the advantage of the patients.

2 *Attitude of positive interest and social 'safety-net' arrangements are essential conditions for stimulating entrepreneurial qualities* Without safety, warmth and recognition it is difficult for the learner to open up for new, unusual behaviours.

3 *Personal articulation of needs by clients and the active creation of social space by sponsors encourages learners to take responsibility* Tension comes from the discrepancy between the situation as experienced and the improvement as envisaged. People with positive energies who see the needs of the client face-to-face, and

who also realize that there is a social space to engage in, are able to embrace this tension as a learning opportunity.

4   *Network relationships enable actors to undertake unusual and unacquainted initiatives* A social network can be characterized as a system of direct contacts and transactions between persons linked together on a voluntary and egalitarian basis. An organization faced with problems for which there are no ready solutions can create fewer limitations by tradition and habit, and more space for unusual dealings if a substantial number of employees have learnt, not only to maintain the going concern in an organized way, but also how to enlarge and enrich networks.

The need to rethink

Since the 1990s there have been extensive mergers and distribution of tasks between hospitals in Austria and Germany with the aim of reducing costs. Hospital managers today are confronted with:

- battlefields of industrial and professional lobbies, distracting attention from the common good and patient care;
- bureaucracy of economic figures, reducing attention to cost reduction and fighting for budgets on formal grounds;
- increasing specialization, blocking sight of the interrelatedness of people within the greater whole;
- ever-growing pressures to keep up with the increasing morbidity due to demographic developments;
- difficulties of financing the seemingly unlimited technological development possibilities;
- great strain on the workforce, leading to demotivation, people leaving organizations and professions, ever more work with less people;
- people are less and less ready to accept what is imposed top-down.

These issues are not new; what is new is their acceleration and aggravation, due to the drastic decline of the financial systems and other environmental factors. This leads to very unstable and volatile situations. How can management achieve sustainable solutions and cooperativeness of the involved parties under these circumstances?

What kind of rethinking is necessary?

A central proposition here is the necessity for working on a general rethinking! Action learning offers the opportunity of reflecting critically on basic assumptions and for working on alternatives in the direction of the mutual cooperation of the professions and disciplines, institutions and organizations. With their heterogeneous memberships, action learning groups offer excellent conditions for challenging existing thoughts, and for learning conversations using the social capital of the involved network within the hospital and with its environment. Five features deserve special attention in any proposed network learning approach:

Five features of network learning

1 *Introductory training* Here participants get a knowledge of the hospital organization and the fields in which it operates. They acquire basic skills for systems thinking, practice reflection and peer coaching and develop an understanding of how to learn and reflect within a network of other people.

2 *Action learning as an integral part of the operating conditions of the organization* Action learning activities are seen as normal work procedures. Employees have a right, and are entitled, to register proposals for improvement and innovation. Proposals are then discussed both locally in their team and also in the top team, enlarged for this purpose by representatives from employees, e.g. the Works Council. If this body agrees to the suggestion, then the employee is mandated to design and execute the action learning project with the help of a high ranking sponsor in the network.

3 *Network dialogues of give and take* Communication between the top team and the various departments is a main avenue for network learning. The top team should meet with departments for structured dialogues on conference outputs about what has been achieved and with what is necessary now. Such dialogues can stimulate an interactional concept of leadership by opening spaces where leaders can fully listen and observe, especially in the questionable situations. Network learning implies a different pattern of interaction from conventional learning. The hierarchy of teacher–pupil relationships gives little chance of role-change, whereas in network learning there is a fundamental equality of all those involved. All are, in any case, learners; and role changes – from coach to coachee, from leader to follower, from adviser to client etc. – are an essential part of the game.

4 *Leadership as a mutual affair* Within the framework of network learning it becomes clear that leadership is a mutual affair. Leaders 'give' direction and those who are led, 'take' or ask for direction. Those who are led also bring forward or 'give' what they are striving for, and where they are taking responsibility, which becomes an

input to the leadership task of helping to clarify goals and means of support.

5   *A long-term orientation* This can be developed by connecting the action learning activities in a series of conferences held every year or so. A first conference could focus on 'community building' where people experience again the richness of their potential for development and are reminded of the value of a common vision. The second conference could elaborate the 'unique selling proposition' of the hospital: where can we contribute best? Where can we complement other hospitals in our direct environment? Costs are reduced and quality increased the more a hospital offers distinct centres of competence which mirror the true strengths of the organization, and joins forces with neighbouring medical facilities in local initiatives such as health centres, nursing homes etc., and with wider ones such as the transition town movement. The focus of the third conference could be 'coping with the course of society' and for aligning the hospital with the ever increasing changes and shifts in society. The repositioning of world powers, climate change and demographic trends are creating fundamentally different conditions. What will the hospital look like in three to five years?

Source: Adapted with permission from Donnenberg (2011: 297–312)

Organizing for the needs of the time

Donnenberg's 'Five features of network learning' contain a vision for an organizing where action learning is not seen as a training tool, but as part of normal work. To achieve this, leadership needs to work with a sense of partnership in a long-term venture. The ambitious action learning adviser can see the ultimate outcome of their work as contributing to this more effective and fulfilling way of working and organizing.

Action learning was conceived to tackle the difficult or 'wicked' problems of organizations and societies. We must worry less about the differences between us in techniques and practices, and focus more on how action learning values can be realized in difficult situations. Revans' own career path points the way, as he moved from physicist to operational researcher to learning practitioner, recognizing the limits of scientific approaches to human problems as he did so. The action learning adviser can contribute to a broader shift of mind, away from people seeing things as puzzles to be solved by existing systems, towards seeking out the problems that never get finally resolved but whose consideration prompts us to new ways of living and working.

As Revans reminds us, action learning is based on ancient wisdom about how to work on the really big challenges in life. The new organizing requires the abilities to self-organize, to share the responsibilities of leadership and to learn together. This is where action learning belongs; in this confluence of the triple practices of leading, organizing and learning (Figure 7.3).

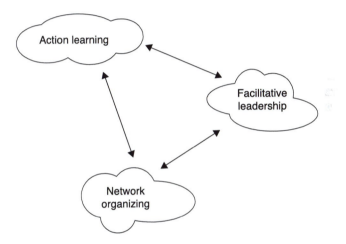

Figure 7.3 An action learning way of working: the triple practices of leading, organizing and learning

My practice notes 7

An action learning way of working

Write some notes on this chapter as it relates to your current practice, and to what you want to do in the future:

(i) What is *my purpose* in action learning? Why am I involved?

(ii) Do I see myself as engaged with developing *facilitative leadership? Does it matter?*

(iii) What opportunities do I see for working with the idea of *partnership working*?

(iv) *Creating knowledge communities* – How could I use my skills here?

(v) *Network organizing* – Is this important to me in my practice?

Reflection on *My practice notes 7*:
Reading through what I have just written, what are my reflections?

8 Developing your practice

Chapter overview

This chapter builds on those earlier to consider the best way of learning to be an action learning adviser. This is a process which may well include training or education but will always require a personal effort at self-development. The idea of practice is central and a model of Knowing, Doing and Being *is offered as a way of framing professional practice. By reflecting on their action and learning a person becomes able to describe their own practice, and to see how it can be improved. The proposed process of development has each person creating the wheel of their own practice through working in a set with other advisers.*

The chapter also touches on the tasks of managing anxiety and power, which are inherent in this role, with some ideas for reducing the former and the need for mindfulness on the latter. The chapter and book conclude with 'the rhythm of professional development' – *the cycle of experiencing, reflecting, reading and writing that characterizes the practice of the action learning practitioner. It is illustrated throughout with extracts from the accounts of practice of new action learning facilitators.*

This chapter contains:

- Introduction
- Becoming an action learning practitioner
- Knowing, Doing and Being
- Anxiety
- Managing your power and anxiety
- The rhythm of professional development: *practice; sharing; reading* and *writing*
- My Practice Notes 8

Introduction

The job of the action learning adviser described in this book is both ambitious and ambiguous, offering exciting opportunities but coming with few prescriptions about how best these can be accomplished.

This is a role more to be learned than to be taught; although there are an increasing number of taught programmes available (see Table 8.1).

Table 8.1 Three approaches to learning to be an action learning adviser

Approach	Description
1: Self-learning, self-development	Individual development of practice, not through a formally taught programme, but using observation, co-facilitation, coaching, reflective practice, reading, writing, etc. Not validated by any external body.
2: Proprietary or private training; usually via a taught programme based on a particular in-house model or approach to action learning	Usually focused on practical aspects of facilitation and methods of practice approved by the programme deliverer or client organization.
	May lead to in-house award, recognized by the awarding organization, for example those of the World Institute of Action Learning (2010) and of Leadership in International Management (2010).
	May be quality assured by an external body against the provider's own curriculum, e.g. as a development programme by the Institute for Leadership and Management (2010). May use logs of practice or mini case studies as evidence for satisfactory attendance and completion.
3: Qualification recognized by a regulatory body; usually a taught programme, against a recognized framework or standard	Generally take a broader approach to understanding the different perspectives on action learning, coupled with critical reflection of own practice, and guided study of underpinning concepts and theory.
	Formally assessed and accredited qualifications, e.g.:
	• standards for action learning facilitators regulated by The Office of Qualifications and Examinations Regulation (2010) and as offered by the Institute for Leadership and Management (ILM) (2010).
	• university accredited programmes that map on to standards set by The Higher Education Academy (2010)

Source: Adapted from Abbott and Boydell (2012)

The growth of the taught programmes reflects a rising demand for action learning which in turn is creating a demand for facilitation. Many aspiring advisers have had their first experience of action learning as set members, and have come to the work with views framed by that experience. However, the recent demand, especially in large organizations, means that others are now coming in from human resources, organization development or service/business improvement backgrounds without necessarily having had that set experience themselves. There is a danger that this will produce trainers not action learners.

Becoming an action learning practitioner

Becoming an action learning practitioner may include the sort of training or education described in approaches 2 and 3 (in Table 8.1), but it will *always* require a self-development approach and a personal effort at learning (as in approach 1).

The case for self-development is partly that it is well nigh impossible to teach this practice but also because this is a role which is chosen not given. As noted in Chapter 4, personal example and commitment are a key part of what is valued in the action learning adviser. The adviser is a practitioner rather a role holder, and this is the sort of work that you have to choose for yourself because the skills and knowledge cannot be separated from the desire to work in this way. If you have this desire then you can learn to fulfill the role, and you will become a better practitioner over time with the help of your friends. Without the desire, this can never happen.

This chapter builds on earlier chapters to offer help in learning to become an action learning adviser: a process which is never complete. Learning to facilitate a set is not like learning to play the piano, for which some training is usually necessary. Anyone can have a go at being the facilitator in an action learning set and the 'first timer' who has just been a set member often makes a surprisingly good job of it (e.g. Lowe 2010). In action learning the new practitioner already has experience of the world, and of other people, and of being in small groups with them (this does not apply so much to the accoucheur and organizational learning roles, although these too must be largely learned from experience). We often recommend the use of 'first timers' in large action learning programmes; on the conditions that (i) these are volunteers who agree to 'have a go'; and (ii) a means is found for supporting their learning in the role.

The idea of practice, discussed below, is central and has several meanings. Developing your practice as an adviser is best done through an action learning process; by working in a set with other colleagues who are also learning their craft. First, a model for thinking about the development of practice: Knowing, Doing and Being (Institute of Leadership and Management (ILM) 2010).

Knowing, doing and being

This is a useful way to think about practice as involving *knowing* (which in the ILM model includes both *declarative knowledge* – the artifacts of knowledge, propositions and sequences of such propositions; and *procedural knowledge* – the productions of declarative knowledge that determine what we do as a result of knowing). *Being* is defined by the ILM in terms of intelligence in a broad sense – which is not an immutable characteristic, but which has multiple facets, is culturally defined and is responsive to social interaction, personality and values. The dynamic between knowing and being influences how we do things (Figure 8.1). At the heart of this model is the mediating function of reflection as personalized in the *reflective practitioner* (Schön 1983). This concept was referred to in Chapters 4 and 6, but here it forms the central idea of how practice is developed.

Reflective practice

> The key to reflection is learning how to take perspective on one's own actions and experience – in other words, to examine that experience rather than just living it. By developing the ability to explore and be curious about our own experience and actions, we suddenly open up the possibilities of purposeful learning – derived not from books or experts, but from our work and our lives.
>
> (Amulya in Reynolds 2011: 8)

Figure 8.1   Knowing, Doing and Being

Source: Based on the original model from ILM and used with permission

As we noted in Chapter 6, reflective practice can be seen as one of three levels of reflection which are of interest to the action learning practitioner (Burgoyne and Reynolds 1997: 1):

- effective practice
- reflective practice
- critically reflective practice

The first of these can be described as technical reflection based on the expert knowledge of the practitioner. We can think of this as a useful type of problem solving. The second category of reflective practice is where ideas are influenced and modified by personal experience to create alternative responses. Schön (1983) pioneered the link between personal experience and reflection in professional development as a corrective to the seemingly dominant approach of 'technical rationality' as practised by the expert. His reflective practitioner was one who not only reflected *on* action but also *in* the midst of action:

- *Reflection-on-action* is carried out after the event, to explore why and how we did what we did; sometimes described as 'hindsight'.
- By connecting feelings and lived experience with awareness of our 'theory-in-use', *reflection-in-action* can be described as 'thinking on one's feet'.

Both aspects of reflective practice are vital in the development of any action learning practitioner. Whilst reflection-on-action helps us to build up a picture of our own professional practice, it is the second aspect of reflection-in-action that builds new understandings that inform our actions in evolving situations. Given the emergent nature of action learning, this takes on a particular value.

However, more recent writers have added a third level of reflection which is increasingly being used to differentiate good practice. As Brookfield points out, *critical reflection* is characterized by a deeper and more intense probing into practice (1995: 8) and is associated with the challenging and controversial idea of emancipation, which has a wide embrace which includes helping someone to free themselves from a restrictive view and provoking direct action by an individual or group.

These levels of reflection can be applied to the Knowing, Doing and Being model (Figure 8.2).

	Initial stage: *Technical reflection*	Development stage: *Reflective practice*	Critical stage: *Critical reflection*
Knowing	The theory of action learning advising . . .	The theory in relation to my practice	The theory in relation to new possibilities for emancipation
Doing	Imitating other action learning advisers	Questioning the rules and methods of action learning	Questioning self and the ends and purposes of action learning
Being	. . . In relation to me as expert practitioner	. . . In relation to me as reflective practitioner	. . . In relation to me as emancipatory practitioner

Figure 8.2   Reflecting on Knowing, Doing and Being

Initial stage: technical reflection

In the initial stage of the development of the person as action learning adviser they are likely to be focused on set advising:

Knowing The new set adviser tends to look for a theory that supports their current position. At this point they will have a number of untested assumptions about the role and the process of action learning itself. This can lead to the conclusion that it is easy and fits all needs and purposes:

'This is the answer to project management training – makes it real.'

'I can see so many ways in which I can incorporate this into my teaching.'

'This method is easy – I don't need to prepare anything, it is "in the moment". The participants do the work.'

'On the programme for facilitation I went on previously we were told that it was a magical process and once we had the magic we could wave our learning wand and all would be well!'

Doing This in-set work can be seductive in that many people will find themselves working in new and creative ways. At this stage people are likely to look for models as they start to develop an understanding of the role. Here are some comments from 'first timers':

'I am going to go back to work and introduce this method on all my programmes.'

'Having to ask the right questions and the structure was quite inhibiting as you're worried you won't get it right, you're thinking so hard about how to phrase the question you don't ask!'

'I want to motivate my set members to be more interactive.'

'I want to start an "on line" action learning set and now need to find a way of doing that.'

Being Sometimes this early experience can leave the adviser so excited by the role that they become true believers and want to get started straight away and spread the word. Alternatively sometimes there is a different reaction – that this isn't new but is a recognition or re-affirmation of previous practice. Either way, the focus tends to be on the self and the individual:

'I felt I had come home.' (in learning)

'This is fantastic . . . an almost magical experience.'

'It was really hard work and I went home shattered but full of ideas.'

'We were active rather than passive recipients of learning.'

'This is like "emperor's new clothes" – we have been doing problem-based learning for years.'

Development stage: reflective practice

In this phase the adviser begins to pull skills, knowledge and theory together and to develop a wider view. Initially, they may be so engrossed in the set facilitator role that they are unaware of the wider setting.

Knowing At this stage the wider role of the set adviser becomes more obvious. After having had some experience of working as set advisers the wider organizational issues appear as practice issues: how can we: 'get buy-in from managers?', 'sell it to the organization?' or 'feedback learning into the company?':

'I am struggling to get buy-in from senior managers.'

'How do I introduce action learning as a way of working?'

'How do you know when the climate in the organization is right to start a set?'

'We have been going through a massive re-organization and I am not sure how action learning will work.'

'Senior managers say they want this [action learning] but I am not sure they know what it is.'

Doing Here the adviser is looking at the rules and methods they have learned and is beginning to question them. During this phase people become aware of differences and have a strong desire to share experiences with other facilitators, to find out what works from others, and to develop their repertoires:

'I have started to trust the set more after all they are the experts in their own work!'

'On reflection, I created a somewhat mechanistic atmosphere of rigid adherence to the philosophy – framed as rules for questioning – which inhibited rather than facilitated the action learning process. Feedback from group members highlighted this.'

'I don't feel I have enough different ways of facilitating the group yet – the more tools and techniques the better.'

'I joined a forum to share ideas and techniques with others.'

'All facilitators should develop the habits of reflection, critique and learning both to ensure the efficacy of the process and to keep themselves honest.'

Being Having internalized the rules, but also begun questioning them, advisers now recognize themselves as reflective practitioners. They begin to free themselves from dependency upon role models and aim for an interdependent relationship to explore each other's learning as peers:

'I have realized that my role is to create a space for the set members that is safe and help them to do the work rather than me trying to do it all.'

'Subconsciously I had in the initial stages as an action learning facilitator actually been part of the problem not part of the solution, in that I found myself slipping into a mentoring role.'

'I have been reflecting on the possibilities offered by Carl Rogers' idea of a facilitator's role as "creating a climate for learning".'

'Reading, thinking and writing about action learning with other people in the set (my comrades in adversity!) and keeping a reflective log have been useful disciplines for me as ways of learning, reflecting, critiquing my practice and acknowledging what I might be doing "right", as well as what I need to do differently.'

'The bigger challenge for me is at the level of building and maintaining networks, communication and sponsorship within the organization. I'm less concerned at this point about how I work within the formal confines of a set, than I am with effectiveness of my communication with the "movers and shakers" and potential set members.'

Critical stage: critical reflection

Questioning the ends and purposes of action learning as well as continuing to question self and practice.

Knowing The theory in relation to new possibilities for emancipation:

'I have become aware how as a manager the organization has influenced and impacted on my value base. Developing as a facilitator it has helped me to develop a critical reflective practice distinguished by questioning assumptions, analysing power relations and being concerned with emancipation and/or empowerment.'

'However, I feel that on reflection we also need to consider, as a small group of facilitators within this team, meeting in the form of facilitators sets in a forum where we would be forever asking ourselves – are we doing it right?'

Doing Questioning self and the ends and purposes of action learning:

'What became very apparent to me as I developed was that what I had been doing as a manager was for the good of the organization, and as a set adviser what I was doing was for the good of the people working in the organization and those it serves – this was quite a revelation to me, and to be honest, liberating for colleagues.'

'I can recognize this in my own practice where work pressures are overwhelming . . . Within this context action learning facilitation is battling against the cynicism of organizational change amongst a culture of highly developed long standing power relations within a group of deputy team managers. Can this be challenged by the facilitator?'

'As an OD Director I implemented change and also had the power to decide what would happen to people if they didn't operate in the way the change required. This caused me all sorts of dilemmas. Using an action learning approach gave me the opportunity to try to give the change back to those people who would be working with it.'

Being In relation to the set adviser as emancipatory practitioner. Embodying authenticity and the potential in my practice:

'I am in a constant struggle with the role of the facilitator as I am aware of my own values and beliefs and I know I prefer to be in control of a situation and leading through a fixed agenda rather than the set taking itself leading through a flexible and more fluid account.'

'I take with me an analysis of power and oppression that takes into account my own matrix of privilege and disadvantage, as well as that of other people.'

'Equally inevitably however, I'm troubled by an inherent contradiction in my attitude towards action learning in as much as – in contrast to the pedagogy of the oppressed – it is first and foremost a tool for education within capitalism, for the improvement of processes and products within an inherently oppressive and exploitative social and economic system.'

The development of the action learning practitioner through these layers of effective practice and reflective practice to critically reflective practice takes commitment, time to experience working with action learning in several settings, and lots of help, support and feedback from friends. This is not a predictable process. Figure 8.2 is of course a model – and like many others in this book not to be mistaken for anyone's actual experience! However, it perhaps illustrates the development path experienced by many advisers.

The knowing, doing and being model can also be utilized as an aid to your reflective practice (Figure 8.3).

Anxiety

The development of your action learning practice through the reflective levels of Knowing, Doing and Being and as outlined in Figure 8.3 is one

Use this after any event or critical incident to reflect on your practice:	
Knowing How does what happened in the set today relate to reading or theoretical framework? What might help my understanding of my work in the set today?	
Doing What do I now want to develop in my practice? What do I intend to do more of or less of in relation to this work?	
Being How was I in my practice today? How do I feel?	

Figure 8.3   Practice review

side of a story. Another side, as prefigured in Chapter 6, is that being an action learning adviser is not just an intellectual activity, but involves strong emotions, the responsible and irresponsible uses of power and 'existential anxiety' (Heron 2008). Everyone who works with action learning experiences this anxiety. It comes in several guises, from not knowing whether they will understand what is happening and make sense of it, to whether they will be accepted or rejected by set members, and especially whether they will manage to be competent and 'do it right'.

All professionals suffer from anxiety because of the discretionary nature of their work, but in action learning, this is compounded by two basic factors. The first stems from Revans' persistent refusal to define it in any single way (which makes it ultimately impossible ever to know whether you are 'doing it right'); the second lies in his warnings about assuming an expert role as a facilitator. This puts the new action learning adviser in a bind: faced by expectant set members who naturally turn to them for definition and rules, the adviser knows that there is no right answer and that she or he should not assume an expert stance: 'Participants' expectations may be that the facilitator is there to reduce anxiety, to lead or teach the group and therefore the role may need clarifying during the programme as neither are compatible with action learning' (Boddy 1981: 4).

There are various ways to deal with this anxiety, but it is not easily avoided. When you think about it, it is an inescapable corollary of Revans' principle of the risk imperative in action learning (2011: 6). And anxiety is in any case endemic in any *learning* approach which is open-ended, unpredictable and emergent. This can be contrasted with a *training* approach, where we constrain the uncertainty and establish order through curricula, 'best practices' and set techniques. Many of us from time to time may find ourselves slipping into training and trying to avoid the anxiety in this way, but this is ultimately a mistake: if there is no one right way to do action learning, then to do it you must also live with the anxiety. Edmonstone (2003) identifies the alternative ways of dealing with anxiety in Figure 8.4.

Reducing *undue* anxiety begins in the accoucheur or initiating role as discussed in Chapter 3. The uncertainties inherent in action learning are likely to be amplified by emergent conditions if it is not set up properly. If some people volunteer to have a go, and others agree to offer support and sponsorship, then this establishes a favourable climate from the outset.

As a set facilitator, taking a SMAL approach as discussed in Chapters 2 and 5 is one way of dealing with the anxiety. An intriguing alternative is to not go to the first meeting of a new set. At the Revans Institute for Action Learning at Salford University all participants were enrolled in sets, and met at least for the first time without any staff present. The set members had to ask each other what they thought they were doing – much as Revans seems to have envisaged it. This made a big difference to any expectations of the staff member, who, attending a second or third meeting, could respond with questions rather than providing inputs. Not being present in a first meeting also makes easier any subsequent withdrawal by the set facilitator.

A good way to start to deal with anxiety is to express it. However, you cannot usually do this with set members if you are in the role of facilitator

Figure 8.4 Alternative routes for anxiety

for obvious reasons – because you are likely to be helping members manage their own anxieties. However, over time the facilitator can show their vulnerability in the set, and indeed this can help the set become less dependent on them. Rush (2002) suggests that the idea of being 'good enough' allows anxiety to be expressed in a way that does not detract from the primary task. This can create a space that 'allows individuals to acknowledge the self and their anxiety in ways which permit and nurture internal and external integration and integrity'.

Perhaps the best source of learning and support for dealing with anxiety can be found in facilitators' sets. These offer the chance to learn through peer supervision as members bring their own facilitating issues to the set. Where facilitators' sets are not available, online networks and associations like IFAL (International Foundation for Action Learning) offer various possibilities. If you have the opportunity of a facilitators' set, this can create a space 'where a reflective mode and a slower pace are promoted and where it is possible to allow vulnerability to surface' (Yelloly and Henkel 1995: 9). Thus anxiety is acknowledged, reflected on and worked with rather than dismissed or repressed.

Managing your power

A parallel and equally unavoidable issue for the action learning practitioner is the question of handling their power. We have mentioned this several times already because of Revans' warnings about the expert facilitator. In Chapter 2 we quoted Dixon's eloquent words on how seductive the power of the 'wise and insightful' set facilitator can be.

Some writers feel that things have changed since Revans' day, and that as most sets have facilitators this is now not really a problem. We don't go along with this; Revans' action learning is a philosophy of peer learning in which each person takes personal responsibility themselves, for their actions and their learning. Facilitators can be very helpful in helping sets to maturity, and being aware of their power and how they are using it is essential not only for staying honest, but also for fulfilling the learning of set members.

In the action learning set, Revans' description of the facilitator as 'supernumary' is a useful corrective to any power they might assume or be given. This is not just because of any seductions of role power or personal prestige, but is crucially important for how members might learn about power and the micropolitics of organizing. In any organizational or social setting, the facilitator would be naive if they imagined that the action learning space is a neutral one free from the replications of existing and previously experienced power relationships.

Whilst a facilitator's set is the best place to discuss these problematic aspects of the adviser's craft, there are useful ways of reflecting alone and recording in your learning journal. After you have had a really good set meeting, or a highly effective meeting with senior managers, or after any other success experience, try Benn's democratic meditation on your powers (Box 8.1).

Box 8.1 Benn's five questions about POWER

If you are advising on action learning, in a set or in an organization, take some time out to reflect on the five questions below. Write down your responses to each before moving on:

1   What power have you got?
2   Where did it come from?
3   In whose interests do you use it?
4   To whom are you accountable?
5   How do we get rid of you?

Read these notes from time to time to remind you of the responsibilities and powers of the action learning adviser. If you have the chance, discuss them with other advisers, and perhaps, if appropriate, with a set.

The rhythm of professional development

We close by drawing attention to the rhythmic cycle of experiencing, reflecting, reading and writing which is part of the life of the practitioner (Figure 8.5). Our experience of working with action learning practitioners matches the well-known Kolb cycle (Kolb et al. 1971: 21–42) and has much in common with many similar models of professional development. In the context of research, Bourner has talked about four ways of knowing: reason or deduction, received knowledge, empiricism and introspection (2002: 2–3); which correspond with the cycle above, which begins with practice (empiricism), and moves round via sharing and sense-making in the set (reason), reading (received knowledge) and writing (introspection).

Practice

Practice is a more useful word for professional development than the over-used competence, which implies ability, but not necessarily action; and

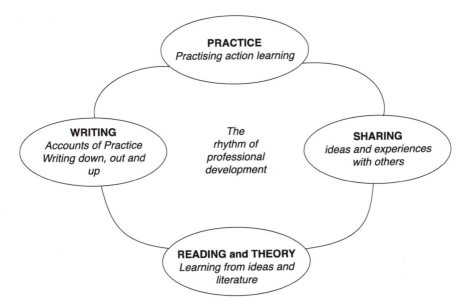

Figure 8.5   The rhythm of professional development

also reflects past learning, but does not suggest the need for anything new. Unlike competence, practice is always situated – it always takes place in a particular setting or context. As Revans caustically observes:

> A man *may well learn to talk about taking action simply by talking about taking action* (as in classes at a business school) but to learn *to take action* (as something distinct from learning to talk about taking action) then he needs *to take action* (rather than to talk about taking action) and to see the effect, not of talking about taking action (at which he may appear competent) but *of taking the action itself* (at which he may fall somewhat short of competent).
>
> (1971: 54–5, original emphases)

The idea of practice means that learning and improving become a normal part of working. This includes one's own personal reflective practice – 'using oneself as data' (Heifetz 1994: 271) – and also working with other people in sets and communities of practice. Practice is also a useful word because it joins up activities that might otherwise become split or mutually exclusive:

Practice connects the person, with a wider group, and to the outer challenges in the world:

- MY practice: my personal way of working
- OUR practice: the professional community of practice
- THE practice: a recognised service for particular human purposes.

(Pedler et al. 2004: 10)

Sharing

In this book we often advocate facilitators' sets, where advisers can have their own space to work on the practice issues as they surface. Facilitators' sets can help with all aspects of the adviser role, starting with issues around initiating action learning, to questions of set facilitation and the art of sharing learning from the sets in the wider social or organizational setting.

The facilitators' set is a shared community of practice on action learning. People offer their accounts of practice in describing what they are doing to help others learn, and to make an impact on the work organization. The set thus forms what Schön called a 'practicum' for developing 'professional artistry' (1987: 16). Like Revans, Schön drew inspiration from Dewey: learners cannot be taught but can be helped to learn: 'He (the learner) has to *see* on his own behalf and in his own way the relations between the means and methods employed and results achieved. Nobody else can see for him, and he can't see just by being "told", although the right kind of telling may guide his seeing and this help him see what he needs to see' (Dewey in Schön 1987: 16–18, original emphasis).

A facilitators' set provides a means for learning about practice through experiment and reflection. But there are also other important ways of learning, including reading about what others have learned, and also in writing about our own discoveries, our own 'accounts of practice'. These accounts can help people to uncover their own 'theories of action' and to detect and correct errors in their practice (Argyris et al. 1987). Becoming aware of our theories of action or internal maps helps us to see where our present assumptions are counterproductive, and then through insightful questioning from colleagues, we may be able to move to new positions which produce better outcomes.

Communities of practice

Communities of practice (CoPs) can be a sort of extended action learning set. According to Lave and Wenger (1991) CoPs encourage members to be involved with one another in action and are therefore much more than membership organizations. CoPs provide a means of bringing together both 'old timers' and 'first timers' to nurture both the individuals and the collective practice.

Action learning communities of practice offer the adviser the opportunity to work on their practice in sets with others. Farley (1986) notes that opening your own practice in this way means exposing your hopes, anxieties, concerns and potential. Action learning CoPs range from the membership network IFAL (International Federation of Action Learning), to Linked-in groups, consultancy networks and other groups either built from past participants in action learning programmes, and from those which have persisted as freestanding sets in their wake after more organized programmes have ended.

Reading

Reading offers new perspectives on familiar situations. As in the set, this activity often leads to personal breakthroughs. A habit of, and a commitment to, reading is a key part of any professional practice as a prime means of integrating new ideas with existing methods to produce new and developing ways of working. Reflecting on work issues and gaining insights from reading can be a powerful experience.

However, reading is often difficult for people, especially where this involves academic material. Just the sight of an academic paper can bring back decades-old flashbacks and remembered humiliations. This is sad because the journals are where new knowledge appears first, and an ability to scan these and read from them selectively is an important aid to the reflective practitioner.

To help with the reading process, it can be very helpful and surprisingly good fun – seriously! – to read a paper with other people. We often ask group members to choose from two or three papers to take away and read on their own, making some notes; and then to come back together with two or three colleagues to pool their learning. In reporting back the highlights from these discussions other members of the group can gain useful insights from their peers, whilst also sharing their own analysis of different papers. This activity not only helps to make people familiar with some key journal papers, but often has very beneficial effects on the readers, raising their confidence levels – and not just where reading is concerned.

Action learners have their own journal, *Action Learning Theory and Practice*, which provides both theoretical perspectives and accounts of practice where practitioners reflect directly on their own practice. A wider literature draws on learning, reflective practice, organizational development and may other connected fields.

Writing

Writing is an important part of professional practice because it facilitates self-reflection and helps the integration of practice and theory. However, like reading, some people may have bad memories of writing perhaps from school, and may need help and encouragement to develop this aspect.

Keeping a personal journal can be a helpful starting point in that it 'focuses on the writer's learning experience itself and attempts to identify the significance and meaning of a given learning experience, primarily for the writer' (Fink 2003: 117). So this may not be too intimidating but it does require discipline, and to get people into the habit it can usefully be built into structures such as programmes or set meetings. Once committed to paper, reflection on and learning from personal journals are often greatly enhanced by sharing personal practice material with trusted colleagues.

The next step in writing is to write up what you have written down in your journal for the benefit of a wider audience. Morris, a colleague of Revans, used to talk about the difference between writing down and writing up. Writing up involves making it readable for other people, which is very different from what you might put in your personal journal. However, as he sagely pointed out, 'you can't write up if you don't write down first'.

The journal *Action Learning Research and Practice* offers a framework for writing of accounts of practice (Box 8.2). This sharing of writing is a good way to engage with the wider action learning community and to enter into an exchange with others. The editors are open to drafts and committed to helping you get them ready for publication.

Box 8.2 Guidelines for an account of practice

Describe the context – where and when this took place

Locate yourself in the story: your role (manager, AL group member, external facilitator . . .); your stake/interest and outcomes you wanted

Purpose of using action learning – expectations and intentions

Who was involved

Your thinking – what action learning ideas have you used and where did this thinking come from? What is the source of these ideas?

Assumptions – why was action learning expected to deliver results in this context?

What happened – how did action learning groups form, what actions were taken, how was learning facilitated, endings, etc.?

Outcomes – what was the result, what worked well, what did not? Why do you think this was?

What insights have you gained?

What lessons are there to share with others?
Source: Adapted from a guide for contributors of *Action Learning Research and Practice* website

If you are thinking of embarking on writing up your account of practice, you might also find the framework in Box 8.3 helpful.

Box 8.3 Zooming in and zooming out

Risner (Knowles and Gilbourne 2010) argues that the process of reflective writing and the 'storying' of reflective experiences can be undertaken around three steps:

1   RETRIEVING THE STORY in words, illustration and movement, looking again at one's life journey, and researching biographical particulars.
2   ZOOMING IN for particular events and issues, looking underneath and between the lines of narrative, reading one's words, shapes, qualities, preferences, energy and imagery.
3   ZOOMING OUT or reading the larger concerns revealed from the uniqueness of the personal narrative. Zooming out for the reflective practitioner allows each narrative reflection to speak again, not merely on a purely personal level, but more broadly in dialogue with critical theories for emancipatory change.

Zooming in and zooming out is a useful way to think about how you can develop what you have first written down. First comes the story, then the search for the critical incidents or moments which illustrate some aspect of practice that we wish to illuminate and reflect upon, and finally the zooming out to see how what we are engaged in is part of a wider context – what or whose purposes are we serving in this work? This stage brings out the critical action learning questions (Chapter 6) where we consider our actions within a wider frame of power dynamics. Here as Russ Vince has said, it is not so much a question of the impact of any action learning on the organization, but rather the impact of the organization on any action learning (2012).

Zooming out is also greatly enhanced by shared or public reflection in the set, where the presence of different perspective contributes to a bigger picture.

 My practice notes 8

Developing my practice

Having thought about your practice as an action learning adviser, what could you do to strengthen your rhythm of professional development? Ask yourself:

1   *Should I think about undertaking some formal study or am I basically happy with the self-development approach?*

2   *What do I do in terms of knowing, doing, and being to promote my own reflective practice, including the aim of becoming a critically reflective practitioner?*

3   *How do I deal with my anxiety in practice?*

4   *How do I manage my power in practice?*

5   *How could I strengthen my rhythm of professional development?*

Reflection on *My practice notes 8*
Reading through what I have just written, what does it say about me and my practice?

References

Introduction

Pedler, M. and Abbott, C. (2008a) Lean and learning: action learning for service improvement, *Leadership in Health Services* 21(2): 87–98.

Pedler, M. and Abbott, C. (2008b) Am I doing it right? Facilitating action learning for service improvement, *Leadership in Health Services* 21(3): 185–99.

Revans, R. (2011) *ABC of Action Learning*. Farnham: Gower.

Chapter 1

Boshyk, Y. (2011) *Ad Fontes* – Reg Revans: some early sources of his personal growth and values, in M. Pedler (ed.) *Action Learning in Practice*, 4th edn. Farnham: Gower.

Boshyk, Y., Barker, A. and Dilworth, R. (2010) Reg Revans: sources of inspiration, practice and theory, in Y. Boshyk and R. Dilworth (eds) *Action Learning: History and Evolution*. Basingstoke: Palgrave Macmillan, pp. 48–72.

Brown, N. (1991) Improving management morale and efficiency, in M.J. Pedler (ed.) *Action Learning in Practice*, 2nd edn. Farnham: Gower, pp. 135–46.

Casey, D. and Pearce, D. (eds) (1977) *More than Management Development: Action Learning at GEC*. Aldershot: Gower.

Clark, P.A. (1972) *Action Research and Organisational Change*. London: Harper & Row.

Coghlan, D. (2011) Practical knowing: the philosophy and methodology of action learning research, in M. Pedler (ed.) *Action Learning in Practice*, 4th edn. Farnham: Gower.

Grint, K. (2008) *Re-thinking D Day*. Basingstoke: Palgrave Macmillan.

Pedler, M. and Abbott, C. (2008) Am I doing it right? Facilitating action learning for service improvement, *Leadership in Health Service*, 21(3): 185–99.

Pedler, M., Burgoyne, J. and Brook, C. (2005) What has action learning learned to become?, *Action Learning: Research & Practice*, 2(1): 49–68.

Revans, R.W. (1971) *Developing Effective Managers*. New York: Praeger.

Revans, R.W. (1980) *Action Learning: New Techniques for Managers*. London: Blond & Briggs.

Revans, R.W. (1982) *The Origins and Growth of Action Learning*. Bromley: Chartwell-Bratt.

Revans, R.W. (2011) *ABC of Action Learning*. Farnham: Gower.

Trehan, K. (2011) Critical action learning, in M. Pedler (ed.) *Action Learning in Practice*, 4th edn. Farnham: Gower, pp. 163–72.

Wieland, G.F. and Leigh, H. (eds) (1971) *Changing Hospitals: A Report on the Hospital Internal Communications Project*. London: Tavistock.

Wieland, G.F. (1981) *Improving Health Care Management*. Ann Arbor, MI: Health Administration Press.

Chapter 2

Beaty, L., Bourner, T. and Frost, P. (1993) Action learning: reflections on becoming a set member, *Management Education and Development*, 24(4): 350–67.

Bourner, T. (2011) Self-managed action learning, in M. Pedler (ed.) *Action Learning in Practice*, 4th edn. Farnham: Gower, pp. 113–324.

Casey, D. and Pearce, D. (eds) (1977) *More than Management Development: Action Learning at GEC*. Aldershot: Gower.

Donnenberg, O. (2011) Network learning in an Austrian hospital – revisited, in M. Pedler (ed.) *Action Learning in Practice*, 4th edn. Farnham: Gower, pp. 297–312.

Marquardt, M. (2004) *Optimizing the Power of Action Learning: Solving Problems and Building Leaders in Real Time*. Palo Alto, CA: Davies-Black.

Marquardt, M. (2009) *Action Learning for Developing Leaders and Organizations: Principles, Strategies, and Cases*. Boston, MA: Nicholas Brealey.

McGill, I. and Beaty, L. (2001) *Action Learning: A Guide for Professional Management and Educational Development*, 2nd edn. London: Kogan Page.

McGill, I. and Brockbank, A. (2004) *The Action Learning Handbook*. London: RoutledgeFalmer.

O'Hara, S., Bourner, T. and Webber, T. (2004) The practice of self-managed action learning, *Action Learning: Research and Practice*, 1(1): 29–42.

Pedler, M., Burgoyne, J. and Brook, C. (2005) What has action learning learned to become?, *Action Learning: Research and Practice*, 2(1): 49–68.

Pedler, M., Burgoyne, J. and Boydell, T. (2010) *A Managers' Guide to Leadership*, 2nd edn. Maidenhead: McGraw-Hill.

Revans, R.W. (1966) *The Theory of Practice in Management*. London: MacDonald.

Revans, R.W. (1971) *Developing Effective Managers*. New York: Praeger.

Revans, R.W. (1980) *Action Learning: New Techniques for Managers*. London: Blond & Briggs.

Revans, R.W. (1982) *The Origins and Growth of Action Learning*. Bromley: Chartwell-Bratt.

Revans, R.W. (2011) *ABC of Action Learning*. Farnham: Gower.

Rigg, C. (2008) Action learning for organizational and systemic development: towards a 'both-and' understanding of 'I' and 'we', *Action Learning: Research & Practice*, 5(2): 105–16.

Chapter 3

Casey, D. (1993) *Managing Learning in Organisations*. Buckingham: Open University Press.

Cho, Y. and Bong, H.C. (2011) Action learning for organisation development in South Korea, in M. Pedler (ed.) *Action Learning in Practice*, 4th edn. Farnham: Gower, pp. 252–3.

Edmonstone, J. (2003) *The Action Learner's Toolkit*. Aldershot: Gower.

McGill, I. and Brockbank, A. (2004) *The Action Learning Handbook*. London: RoutledgeFalmer.

Nicolini, D., Sheer, M., Childerstone, S. and Gorli, M. (2004) In search of the structure that reflects: promoting organisational reflective practices in a UK health authority, in M. Reynolds and R. Vince (eds) *Organising Reflection*. Aldershot: Ashgate, pp. 81–104.

Pedler, M. (2003) *The Action Learning Toolkit*. Ely: Fenman.

Pedler, M. (2008) *Action Learning for Managers*. Farnham: Gower, pp. 20–2.

Revans, R.W. (1971) *Developing Effective Managers*. New York: Praeger.

Revans, R.W. (1982) *The Origins and Growth of Action Learning*. Bromley: Chartwell-Bratt.

Revans, R.W. (2011) *ABC of Action Learning*. Farnham: Gower.

Chapter 4

Casey, D. (2011) David Casey on the role of the set adviser, in M. Pedler (ed.) *Action Learning in Practice*, 4th edn. Farnham: Gower, pp. 55–70.

Caulat, G. (2006) Virtual leadership, *The Ashridge Journal*, Autumn.

Caulat, G. (2012) *Virtual Leadership: Learning to Lead Differently*. Faringdon: Libri.

Caulat, G. and De Haan, E. (2006) Virtual peer consultation: how virtual leaders learn, *Organizations and People*, 13: 24–32.

Dickinson, M., Burgoyne, J. and Pedler, M. (2010) Virtual action learning: practices and challenges, *Action Learning: Research and Practice*, 7(1): 59–72.

Edmonstone, J. (2003) *The Action Learner's Toolkit*. Aldershot: Gower.

Heron, J. (1999) *The Facilitator's Handbook*. London: Kogan Page.

Lowe, K. (2010) Introducing action learning in local government: a new facilitator's experience, *Action Learning: Research and Practice*, 7(1): 83–7.

Marshall, J. (2001) Self-reflective inquiry practices, in P. Reason and H. Bradbury (eds) *Handbook of Action Research*. London: Sage, pp. 433–9.

Mead, G. (2006) Developing public service leaders through action inquiry, in C. Rigg and S. Richards (eds), *Action Learning, Leadership and Organisational Development in Public Services*. Abingdon: Routledge, pp. 155–64.

O'Hara, S., Bourner, T. and Webber, T. (2004) The practice of self managed action learning, *Action Learning: Research & Practice*, 1(1): 29–42.

Owen, H. (1997) *Open Space Technology*. San Francisco, CA: Berrett-Koehler.

Pedler, M. (2008) *Action Learning for Managers*. Farnham: Gower.

Pedler, M., Burgoyne, J. and Brook, C. (2005) What has action learning learned to become?, *Action Learning: Research and Practice*, 2(1): 49–68.

Pedler, M. and Abbott, C. (2008) Am I doing it right?, *Leadership In Health Services*, 21(3): 185–99.

Revans, R.W. (2011) *ABC of Action Learning*. Farnham: Gower.

Revans, R.W. (1982) Management productivity and risk – the way ahead, in *The Origins and Growth of Action Learning*. London: Chartwell Bratt, pp. 693–717.

Shepherd, C. (2011) *The New Learning Architect*. www.onlignment.com/newlearningarchitect (accessed 7 September 2012).

Weaver, R. and Farrell, J. (1997) *Managers as Facilitators: A Practical Guide to Getting Things Done in the Workplace*. San Francisco, CA: Berrett-Koehler.

Wilson, O. (2010) From practise to practice: action learning to support Transforming Derby, *Action Learning: Research and Practice*, 7(3): 287–95.

Chapter 5

Argyris, C. and Schön, D. (1978) *Organizational Learning: A Theory of Action Perspective*. Reading, MA: Addison Wesley.

Attwood, M., Pedler, M., Pritchard, S. and Wilkinson, D. (2003) *Leading Change: A Guide to Whole Systems Working*. Bristol: Policy Press.

Bourner, T. (2011) Self-managed action learning, in M. Pedler (ed.) *Action Learning in Practice*, 4th edn. Farnham: Gower, pp. 113–24.

Department of Health/Pathology Modernisation (2008) *Action for Change: Transforming Pathology Services through Action Learning*, November.

Garratt, R. (1990) *Creating a Learning Organisation*. London: Director Books.

Murphy, L. (2003) Leading the development of a learning organisation. Unpublished dissertation presented in part-fulfilment of the requirements of an MA in Change Management at the University of Brighton, Brighton Business School, University of Brighton.

Revans, R.W. (2011) *ABC of Action Learning*. Farnham: Gower.

Senge, P. (1990) *The Fifth Discipline: The Art and Practice of the Learning Organization*. New York: Doubleday Currency.

Tamkin, P. (2000) The impact of whole person development schemes on managers. Unpublished PhD dissertation, University of Brighton.

Wilhelm, W. (2005) *Learning Architectures: Building Individual and Organizational Learning*. New Mexico: GCA Press.

Chapter 6

Adams, G. and Balfour, D. (1998) *Unmasking Administrative Evil*. London: Sage.

Alvesson, M. and Willmott, H. (1996) *Making Sense of Management: A Critical Introduction*. London: Sage.

Anderson, L. and Thorpe, R. (2004) New perspectives on action learning: developing criticality, *Journal of European Industrial Training*, 28(8/9): 657–68.

Attwood, M., Pedler, M., Pritchard, S. and Wilkinson, D. (2003) *Leading Change: A Guide to Whole Systems Working*. Bristol: Policy Press.

Attwood, M. (2007) Challenging from the margins into the mainstream – improving renal services in a collaborative and entrepreneurial spirit, *Action Learning Research and Practice*, 4(2): 191–8.

Banister, D. and Fransella, F. (1971) *Inquiring Man: The Theory of Personal Constructs*. Harmondsworth: Penguin.

Brookfield, S. (1987) *Developing Critical Thinkers: Challenging Adults to Explore Alternative Ways of Thinking and Acting*. Milton Keynes: Open University Press.

Brookfield, S. (1994) Tales from the Dark Side: a phenomenology of adult critical reflection, *International Journal of Lifelong Education*, 13: 203–16.

Brookfield, S. (2011) 'Critical Perspectives' talk given to ESRC seminar: The promises and problems of critical reflection, University of Birmingham, 30 June.

Burgoyne, J. and Reynolds, M. (eds) (1997) *Management Learning: Integrating Perspectives in Theory and Practice*. London: Sage.

Myerson, D.E. (2003) *Tempered Radicals: How Everyday Leaders Inspire Change at Work*. Boston: Harvard Business School Press.

Myerson, D. and Scully, M. (1995) Tempered radicals and the politics of radicalism and change, *Organization Science*, 6(5): 585–600.

Raelin, J. (2008) Emancipatory discourse and liberation, *Management Learning*, 39(5): 519–40.

Revans, R.W. (1971) *Developing Effective Managers*. New York: Praeger.

Revans, R.W. (1982) *The Origins and Growth of Action Learning*. Bromley: Chartwell-Bratt.

Revans, R.W. (2011) *ABC of Action Learning*. Aldershot: Gower.

Reynolds, M. (1998) Reflection and critical reflection in management learning, *Management Learning*, 29(2): 183–200.

Reynolds, M. and Vince, R. (2004) Critical management education and action-based learning: synergies and contradictions, *Academy of Management Learning and Education*, 3(4): 442–56.

Rigg, C. and Trehan, K. (2008) Critical reflection in the workplace: is it just too difficult? *Journal of European Industrial Training*, 32(5): 374–84.

Trehan, K. and Pedler, M. (2009) Animating critical action learning; process-based leadership and management development, *Action Learning Research and Practice*, 6(1): 35–49.

Vince, R. (2002) Organizing Reflection, *Management Learning*, 33(1): 63–78.

Vince, R. (2004) Action learning and organizational learning: power, politics and emotions in organizations, *Action Learning Research and Practice*, 1(1): 63–78.

Vince, R. (2008) 'Learning-in-action' and learning inaction: advancing the theory and practice of critical action learning, *Action Learning Research and Practice*, 5(2): 93–104.

Vince, R. (2011) Critical action learning, IFAL: *Action Learning News*, September.

Watson, T. (1994) *In Search of Management*. London: Routledge.

Willmott, H. (1994) Management education: provocations to a debate, *Management Learning*, 25(1): 105–36.

Willmott, H. (1997) Making learning critical: identity, emotion and power in processes of management development, *Systems Thinking*, 10(6): 749–71.

Chapter 7

Adams, D. and Dixon, N. (1997) Action learning at Digital Equipment, in M. Pedler (ed.) *Action Learning in Practice*, 3rd edn. Aldershot: Gower, pp. 129–38.

Coughlan, P. and Coghlan, D. (2011) *Collaborative Strategic Improvement through Network Action Learning*. Cheltenham: Edward Elgar.

Cross, R. and Parker, A. (2004) *The Hidden Power of Social Networks: Understanding How Work Really Gets Done in Organizations*. Boston, MA: Harvard Business Press.

Donnenberg, O. (2011) Network learning in an Austrian hospital, in M. Pedler (ed.) *Action Learning in Practice*. Farnham: Gower, pp. 297–312.

Doz, I. and Hamel, G. (1998) *Alliance Advantage: The Art of Creating Value through Partnering*. Boston, MA: Harvard Business School Press.

Hamel, G. (2012) published extract from *What Happens Now: How to Win in a World of Relentless Change* (Chichester: Wiley), *The Guardian*, 10 March 2012.

Johnson, C. (2010) A framework for the ethical practice of action learning, *Action Learning: Research & Practice*, 7(3): 267–83.

Pedler, M. (2011) *Facilitating Leadership through Action Learning: The Case of the Creative and Cultural Industries*. Final Report to ALA/CLP on the CLP Leadership Facilitation Skills Programme 2008–10, January.

Pedler, M. and Attwood, M. (2011)) How can action learning contribute to social capital?, *Action Learning: Research & Practice*, 8(1): 27–40.

Raelin, J. (2003) *Creating Leaderful Organizations: How to Bring out Leadership in Everyone*. San Francisco, CA: Berrett-Koehler.

Revans, R.W. (1971) *Developing Effective Managers*. New York: Praeger.

Revans, R.W. (1980) *Action Learning: New Techniques for Management*. London: Blond & Briggs.

Revans, R.W. (1982) *The Origins and Growth of Action Learning*. Bromley: Chartwell-Bratt.

Revans, R.W. (2011) *ABC of Action Learning*. Farnham: Gower.

Venner, K. (2009) Facilitative leadership, in *The Action Learning Handbook*. London: Action Learning Associates.

Willis, V. (2004) Inspecting cases against Revans' 'gold standard' of action learning, *Action Learning: Research & Practice*, 1(1): 11–27.

Chapter 8

Abbott, C. and Boydell, T. (2012) Learning to be an action learning facilitator: three approaches, in M. Pedler (ed.) *Action Learning in Practice*, 4th edn. Farnham: Gower, pp. 273–84.

Argyris, C., Putnam, R. and Smith, D. (1987) *Action Science*. San Francisco, CA: Jossey-Bass.

Boddy, D. (1981) Putting action learning into action, *Journal of European Industrial Training*, 5(5): 2–20.

Brookfield, S.D. (1995) *Becoming a Critically Reflective Teacher*. San Francisco, CA: Jossey Bass.

Bourner, T. (2002) Practitioner research and the PhD. Seminar given in the series *New Directions in Action Learning*, University of Salford, UK: Revans Institute for Action Learning and Research, 28 September 2000.

Burgoyne, J. and Reynolds, M. (eds) (1997) *Management Learning: Integrating Perspectives in Theory & Practice*. London: Sage.

Edmonstone, J. (2003) *The Action Learner's Toolkit*. Aldershot: Gower.

Farley, M. (1986) *Personal Commitments*. San Francisco, CA: Harper and Row.

Fink, L.D. (2003) *Creating Significant Learning Experiences: An Integrated Approach to Designing College Courses*. San Francisco, CA: Jossey-Bass.

Heifetz, R. (1994) *Leadership Without Easy Answers*. Cambridge, MA: Belknap Press.

Heron, J. (2008) *The Facilitator's Handbook*. London: Kogan Page.

Institute of Leadership and Management (2010) *Index of Leadership Trust*. London: Institute of Leadership and Management.

Institute of Leadership and Management (2010) http://www.i-l-m.com/downloads/resources/centres/qualification-specifications/ (accessed 7 September 2012).

Knowles, Z. and Gilbourne, D. (2010) Aspiration, inspiration and illustration: initiating debate on reflective practice writing, *The Sport Psychologist*, 24: 504–20.

Kolb, D., Rubin, I. and McIntyre, J. (1971) *Organizational Psychology: An Experiential Approach*. Englewood Cliffs, NJ: Prentice-Hall.

Lave, J. and Wenger, E. (1991) *Situated Learning: Legitimate Peripheral Participation*. Cambridge: Cambridge University Press.

Leadership in International Management (2010) https://www.milinstitute.se

Lowe, K. (2010) Introducing action learning in local government: a new facilitator's experience, *Action Learning: Research and Practice*, 7(1): 83–7.

Pedler, M., Burgoyne, J. and Boydell, T. (2004) *A Manager's Guide to Leadership*. Maidenhead: McGraw-Hill.

Qualifications and Examinations Regulation (2010) http://register.ofqual.gov.uk/Qualification/Details/501_0901_7 (accessed 7 September 2012).

Revans, R. (1971) *Developing Effective Managers*. New York: Praeger.

Revans, R. (2011) *ABC of Action Learning*. Farnham: Gower.

Reynolds, M. (2011) Reflective practice: origins and interpretations, *Action Learning Research and Practice*, 8(1): 5–13.

Rush, G. (2002) From triangle to spiral: reflective practice in social work education, practice and research, *Social Work Education*, 21(2).

Schön, D. (1983) *The Reflective Practitioner*. New York: Basic Books.

Schön, D. (1987) *Educating the Reflective Practitioner: Towards a New Design for Teaching and Learning in the Professions*. San Francisco, CA: Jossey Bass.

The Higher Education Academy (2010) http://www.heacademy.ac.uk/

Vince, R. (2012) The impact of action learning, keynote address to the International Action Learning Conference, Ashridge Management School, Berkhamstead, 2–4 April.

World Institute of Action Learning (2010) http://www.wial.org/getCertified/ALCertificationRequirements.pdf (accessed 7 September 2012).

Yelloly, M. and Henkel, M. (eds) (1995) *Learning and Teaching in Social Work: Towards Reflective Practice*. London: Jessica Kingsley.

Validated by

Action learning facilitation

ILM is delighted to validate *Facilitating Action Learning* by Mike Pedler and Christine Abbott. We believe the book is an ideal course reader for anyone taking the ILM Level 5 Certificate and Diploma qualifications in Action Learning Facilitation.

Action learning is a technique used primarily in leadership and management development and is based on the simple idea that leaders and managers learn best by working together in a group, helping each other to find solutions to real work problems through discussion.

Our qualifications are designed to train learning and development professionals in the role of the action learning facilitator: to provide guidance to the group, ensure that it adheres to basic principles and to enable access to expert knowledge. Mike Pedler and Christine Abbott's book is practice focused and focuses on developing practitioners' confidence in their ability to facilitate action learning sets. As such, it fits the ILM vision and aids our learner's journey.

Overview of ILM

ILM is the largest independent organization focused on leadership and management. We support organizations in building strong leaders and managers through qualifications, membership and CPD support.

We offer more leadership and management qualifications than any other awarding body through our network of 2500 accredited centres worldwide. Not only are our qualifications industry-standard, ranging from team leader programmes to diplomas for senior directors, but they help retain and motivate staff too. There are over 130 programmes to choose from: diplomas in leadership through to team leading awards and certificates in coaching.

We also connect a community of 35,000 leaders and managers committed to making a real difference to their organizations. They have become better managers by receiving the professional recognition and management support that comes with ILM membership.

Through real-life application and independent research, we know what makes a good manager and a motivating leader. We are passionate about the difference good leadership and management make to individual and organizational success.

ILM:

- accredits 2,500 training providers and colleges;
- connects a community of 35,000 managers;
- has a portfolio of over 130 leadership and management qualifications;
- endorses employer in-house programmes;
- accredits training providers;
- commissions independent research.

www.i-l-m.com

THE MANAGEMENT MAP

Manager level	Key competencies	Membership grade	Qualification level (VRQs)	Academic equivalent
CEO and director of large divisions	• Lead senior management team; provide vision and direction for the organization (CEO only) • Provide organizational leadership; build commitment to the vision and values. Develop corporate policy and strategy, lead change, optimize organizational capacity, develop excellence and a customer-focused approach; ensure long-term financial stability and growth. **Underpinned by** critical thinking and research, ability to make hard decisions and solve 'wicked' problems. Knows strategic issues of function specific areas (HR, Marketing, Finance, Operations, R&D)	Fellow	7	Post-graduate degree

(Continued)

Manager level	Key competencies	Membership grade	Qualification level (VRQs)	Academic equivalent
Senior manager (departmental/ divisional/ functional manager in larger organizations)	• Provide departmental leadership; plan and implement strategies; lead change programmes. • Plan and manage operations, people and resources to maximize effectiveness; monitor performance and control budgets • Encourage innovation, effective internal communications and cross-functional/ inter-departmental working; assess and manage risks and contingency planning **Underpinned by** information analysis and synthesis, financial and performance management skills, and understands key operational issues in function-specific areas (HR, Marketing, Finance, Operations, R&D, etc.)	Member or Fellow	6/7	Degree – full and post-graduate degree
Manager – departmental/ divisional/ functional manager – in medium-sized organizations; intermediate/ middle manager in larger organization	• Provide departmental/divisional leadership; plan, manage, and monitor operations; lead change projects; develop people and resources to maximize operational safety, efficiency and effectiveness; monitor performance and control budgets	Member	4/5	Up to second year of degree, Foundation Degree or HND

	Encourage innovation and improvement, set goals and delegate tasks to direct reports, communicate with teams and manage risks **Underpinned by** information analysis, financial, people and performance management skills; and an awareness of key issues in other areas (HR, Marketing, Finance, Operations, R&D)			
First line manager/ supervisor	• Provide leadership to an operational or functional team; plan and manage workload; communicate plans and objectives and build engagement; manage individual and team performance and development; encourage innovation, support and lead change projects; initiate and lead improvement **Underpinned by:** self-management, team building and performance management skills; information processing skills; an awareness of customers and their requirements, organizational policies and procedures, and inter-personal dynamics	Associate	3	A Level

(Continued)

Manager level	Key competencies	Membership grade	Qualification level (VRQs)	Academic equivalent
Team supervisor/ team leader	• Provide leadership to a team; plan day-to-day workload, and allocate, and monitor tasks, resolve problems, support change, brief and motivate a team. **Underpinned by:** self-management and team building skills; aware of customers' requirements, and inter-personal dynamics	Affiliate	2	GCSE

*NB: Higher level leadership roles imply possession of the knowledge and skills of lower level roles.

Subject index

Author index

A MANAGER'S GUIDE TO SELF DEVELOPMENT
Fifth Edition

Mike Pedler, John Burgoyne
and Tom Boydell

9780077114701 (Paperback)
2006

eBook also available

A Manager's Guide to Self-Development has become the
indispensable guide for building management skills. Now in its fifth
edition the book details a self-development programme aimed at
helping readers improve their managerial performance, advance their
careers and realize their full potential.

Key features:

- 6 new activities including find a mentor, be a good coach, treat
  yourself well, coping with difficult situations, effective
  communication styles, and multiple intelligence
- Simplified diagnostic exercise to help you identify which are the
  best activities for you to follow
- Updated references and follow up activities throughout

www.openup.co.uk

OPEN UNIVERSITY PRESS
McGraw - Hill Education